Y0-BOE-298

M·E·N·U · M·A·S·T·E·R·S

INDIAN COOKERY

EDITED BY
RACHEL GRENFELL

OCTOPUS BOOKS

MENU MATCH CODE

To allow more flexibility within the menus we have added bold numbers after certain recipes to offer suitable alternatives.

Thus, if the numbers ·3·11·14· appear after a starter, they indicate that the starter of Menu 3, 11, or 14 could be substituted.

Using the MENU MATCH CODE you will be sure to find a menu to suit all tastes.

NOTES

Standard spoon measurements are used in all recipes
1 tablespoon – one 15 ml spoon
1 teaspoon – one 5 ml spoon
All spoon measures are level
Where amounts of salt and pepper are not specified, the cook should use her own discretion.
Canned foods should not be drained, unless so stated in the recipe. For all recipes, quantities are given in metric, imperial and American measures. Follow one set of measures only, because they are not interchangeable.

Jacket Photograph: Tandoori Chicken, Kitcheri, Naan Bread, Chick-Pea Fudge

First published 1986 by
Octopus Books Limited
59 Grosvenor Street, London W1

© 1986 Octopus Books Limited

ISBN 0 7064 2541 3

Produced by Mandarin Publishers Ltd
22a Westlands Rd
Quarry Bay, Hong Kong
Printed in Hong Kong

C · O · N · T · E · N · T · S

I·N·T·R·O·D·U·C·T·I·O·N

Even the most confident of cooks can become stuck for new ideas or pale at the prospect of entertaining family and friends. What to cook? How much to prepare in advance? How to make sure everything arrives at the table on time?

Menu Masters Indian Cookery provides the answers with easy-to-follow imaginative menus and all the forward planning is done for you. Detailed preparation notes with a countdown to serving will take you through each stage of the way to a relaxed, hitch-free meal.

Indian food lends itself to many occasions – from formal dinners to casual family suppers. It must be one of the simplest ways to entertain.

To say "we had a curry last night" is a common understatement. Indian cuisine is extremely versatile, offering a great deal more to experience than 'curry'. In its most diverse form an Indian meal consists of bread, rice, meat or poultry, dal, vegetables, raita, chutney and possibly a dessert, although sweet dishes are normally eaten at teatime or as a snack.

As there is no meat-and-two-vegetables tradition in Indian food menus have been carefully compiled from the wide spectrum of Indian dishes. Each one balanced in colour, texture and flavour. Many of the recipes are more fragrant than hot and spicy and so even the most wary of diners will be pleasantly surprised.

Preparation and freezer notes are provided indicating which dishes can be made and frozen well in advance. Nearly all Indian food can be prepared ahead.

⋰M⋅E⋅N⋅U⋱

· 1 ·

Cocktail Snacks for 8 to 10

Samosas
Potato Bondas
Pakoras
Vegetable Pakoras

Cocktail Accompaniments

For a cocktail party with a difference, serve Indian snacks and savouries. These are a speciality of Indian cuisine. No evening walk or visit to friends is complete without a snack – a handful of freshly roasted split peas (*channa*), spicy deep-fried samosas, crisp pakoras or any of the dozens of titbits that comprise the repertoire.

Traditionally served with tea, coffee, sherbets (page 48) or soft drinks, these snacks are ideal accompaniments for alcoholic drinks too.

Varying the Fillings

Samosas are most commonly made with a vegetable stuffing. Try using potatoes or a mixture of potatoes and peas instead of the meat. Boil the vegetables, then fry them with the onion and other ingredients. Season well and, if you like pungent food, do not discard the seeds of the chilli.

Pakoras are savoury fritters made from a thick batter. Sometimes just the batter is deep-fried but it is often used to coat vegetables. Potatoes and cauliflower are used in this menu, although sliced onions and spinach leaves are very good, too. The flour used to make the batters is chick pea flour (*besan*); it is available in all Indian or Pakistani food stores and in some health food shops.

Chutney makes a good accompaniment to these savouries. Or, try a spicy tomato ketchup – just stir a little cayenne into the ketchup.

Samosas

Metric/Imperial	American
150 g/5 oz plain flour	1¼ cups all-purpose flour
pinch of salt	pinch of salt
¼ teaspoon baking powder	¼ teaspoon baking powder
25 g/1 oz butter or ghee (page 8)	2 tablespoons butter or ghee (page 8)
water to mix	water to mix
Filling:	Filling:
15 g/½ oz ghee or 1 tablespoon oil	1 tablespoon ghee or oil
1 onion, chopped	1 onion, chopped
250 g/8 oz lean meat, very finely minced	1 cup very finely ground lean meat
salt	salt
freshly ground black pepper	freshly ground black pepper
1 green chilli, seeded and very finely chopped	1 green chili, seeded and very finely chopped
2-3 sprigs coriander leaves, chopped	2-3 sprigs coriander leaves, chopped
juice of ½ lemon	juice of ½ lemon
Flour Paste:	Flour Paste:
2-3 teaspoons plain flour mixed with a little water	2-3 teaspoons all-purpose flour mixed with a little water
oil, for deep-frying	oil, for deep-frying

1. Sift the flour, salt and baking powder into a bowl. Rub (cut) in the butter or ghee. Add enough water to make a soft smooth dough. Cover and set aside.
2. To make the filling, heat the ghee or oil in a saucepan and lightly sauté the onion. Add the meat and salt and pepper. Add a little water and gently sauté the meat, stirring occasionally, for 10 to 12 minutes until dry. Add the chilli, coriander and lemon juice and mix well. Remove from the heat and allow to cool.
3. Meanwhile, knead the dough well and divide into 16 to 18 even-sized balls. Flatten each ball, dust with flour and roll out into a 10-13 cm/4-5 inch round. Cut across the centre to make two half moons. Apply a little of the flour paste down the straight edge and bring the two corners together to make a cone, gently pressing the pasted edges together to secure. Shape the rest of the dough in the same way.
4. Fill the cone with a little of the filling, apply flour paste to the top edge of the cone and seal the shape. Prepare the remaining samosas in a similar manner.
5. Heat the oil in a deep-fryer to 190°C/375°F or until a cube of bread browns in 30 seconds. Deep-fry the samosas, a few at a time, until they are golden brown. Drain on absorbent kitchen paper and serve while still warm.

Potato Bondas

Metric/Imperial	American
125 g/4 oz chick pea flour (besan)	generous 1 cup chick pea flour (besan)
salt	salt
pinch of baking powder	pinch of baking powder
½ teaspoon chilli powder	½ teaspoon chili powder
about 150 ml/¼ pint water	about ⅔ cup water
Filling:	Filling:
500 g/1 lb potatoes, boiled, peeled and cubed	1 lb potatoes, boiled, peeled and cubed
2 green chillis, seeded and very finely chopped	2 green chilis, seeded and very finely chopped
15 g/½ oz fresh root ginger, peeled and chopped	½ oz fresh gingerroot, peeled and chopped
1 small onion, finely chopped	1 small onion, finely chopped
2 sprigs coriander leaves, chopped	2 sprigs coriander leaves, chopped
salt	salt
freshly ground black pepper	freshly ground black pepper
1 tablespoon lemon juice	1 tablespoon lemon juice
	oil, for deep-frying

1. Sift the chick pea flour, salt and baking powder into a bowl. Add the chilli powder and sufficient water to make a smooth batter. Beat well, then set aside.

2. To make the filling, mix together the potato, chilli, ginger, onion, coriander leaves, salt and pepper. Stir in the lemon juice and mix thoroughly. With wet hands, divide the filling into about 20 small balls. Dip these in the batter.

3. Heat the oil in a deep-fryer until a drop of the batter rises quickly to the surface and turns crisp. Deep-fry the bondas a few at a time, until golden brown. Drain well on absorbent kitchen paper. Serve hot or warm.

Pakoras

Metric/Imperial
125 g/4 oz chick pea flour
  (besan)
½ teaspoon chilli powder

American
1 cup chick pea flour
  (besan)
½ teaspoon chili powder

½ teaspoon salt
150 ml/¼ pint natural
  yogurt
1 teaspoon lemon juice
oil, for deep-frying

½ teaspoon salt
⅔ cup unflavored yogurt
1 teaspoon lemon juice
oil, for deep-frying

1. Sift the flour into a bowl, rubbing any lumps through a sieve (strainer) with the back of a spoon. Add the chilli powder and salt and mix well. Gradually stir in the yogurt and lemon juice. Cover and leave in a cool place for 2 hours until the batter is thick; it should be much thicker than a pancake (crêpe) batter.

2. Heat the oil in a deep-fryer until a drop of the batter sizzles and rises to the surface. Drop in spoonfuls of the batter and fry until golden. Drain on crumpled greaseproof (waxed) paper or absorbent kitchen paper. Serve fresh and warm.

A selection of cocktail snacks: Samosas; Potato bondas; Pakoras

Vegetable Pakoras

Metric/Imperial	American
175 g/6 oz plain or chick pea flour (besan)	1½ cups all-purpose flour or chick pea flour (besan)
½ teaspoon salt	½ teaspoon salt
½ teaspoon bicarbonate of soda	½ teaspoon baking soda
½ teaspoon ground coriander seeds	½ teaspoon ground coriander seeds
½ teaspoon ground turmeric	½ teaspoon ground turmeric
½ teaspoon ground cumin	½ teaspoon ground cumin
¾ teaspoon whole lovage (ajwain) seeds (optional)	¾ teaspoon whole lovage (ajwain) seeds (optional)
1 teaspoon freshly ground black pepper	1 teaspoon freshly ground black pepper
300 ml/½ pint water	1¼ cups water
oil, for deep-frying	oil, for deep-frying
1 medium potato, peeled and sliced	1 medium potato, peeled and sliced
1 small cauliflower, broken into florets	1 small cauliflower, broken into flowerets

1. Sift the flour, salt and bicarbonate of soda (baking soda) into a bowl. Add the spices, then slowly whisk in the water to make a smooth batter.
2. Heat the oil in a deep-fryer to 190°C/350°F or until a cube of bread browns in 30 seconds.
3. Dip the potato slices in the batter to coat thoroughly, shaking off any excess. Deep-fry until golden-brown and crisp. Remove with a slotted spoon and drain on absorbent kitchen paper.
4. Coat and fry the cauliflower in the same way. Serve the pakoras hot or warm.

Ghee

Ghee is a kind of clarified butter. Like clarified butter, it does not burn so easily as butter, enabling cooking at higher temperatures. You can buy ghee at Asian grocers or make it at home. To make ghee: melt 250 g/8 oz (1 cup) unsalted butter in a small saucepan over low heat. Cook just below simmering point for 20 to 30 minutes or until all the water in the butter has evaporated and the liquid is beginning to change colour. You can tell when this stage is reached because it will stop spluttering. Remove from the heat and strain through two or three thicknesses of muslin (cheesecloth). Pour the ghee into a screw-top jar, shut tightly and store in a cool place. Refrigeration is unnecessary.

Optional Extra:

Serve a variety of chutneys with the snacks given in this menu. Try some of the following: banana chutney (page 12), apricot chutney (page 28), mango chutney (page 32) and apple chutney (page 56). Or try tomato and yogurt relish (page 35).

C · O · U · N · T · D · O · W · N

On the day:

Prepare the samosa pastry (dough), cover and store in the refrigerator. Make up the samosa filling. Prepare the bonda filling and roll into balls. Make up the batter. Cover both and refrigerate. Make the vegetable pakora batter. Prepare the potatoes and cauliflower, cover with cold water.

To serve at 6.30 pm:

4.00: Make the pakora batter. Cover and leave in a cool place.
4.15: Finish shaping and filling the samosas.
5.15: Chill any drinks.
5.45: Deep-fry the samosas, drain and keep warm.
6.00: Coat the bondas and vegetable pakoras in batter. Deep-fry, drain and keep warm. Deep-fry spoonfuls of pakora batter. Drain and keep warm.
6.30: Serve the drinks and snacks.

F · R · E · E · Z · E · R · N · O · T · E · S

Freeze the samosas and bondas after shaping and filling. Open freeze on trays, then pack in rigid containers or polythene (plastic) bags. Freeze for up to 3 months. Deep-fry from frozen.

⠹M⸱E⸱N⸱U⠹

· 2 ·

Weekend Dinner for 4

Lamb Curry with Cracked Wheat
Sour-sweet Chick Peas
Spicy Turnips
Aubergine and Potatoes
Banana Chutney

Balanced, well flavoured and easy to prepare, this menu is ideal for weekend entertaining. The lamb and cracked wheat can be prepared the day before and reheated before serving, avoiding any last minute panics for the cook.

Cracked wheat is sold in most health food shops. If it is not available use a mixture of oats, barley and split peas.

A Nutritious Pulse

Sour-sweet chick peas are commonly eaten as a snack in India but may also be served as part of a meal. Chick peas provide valuable protein, especially for vegetarians. Tamarind, the seed pod of a tropical tree, is used in this recipe. The pulp from the pod acts as a souring agent. Tamarind is available in Indian and South-East Asian food stores as pulp and pods. Both kinds must be soaked in hot water for 10 to 15 minutes, then pushed through a strainer. Use the pulpy liquid and discard the seeds and fibres. The Banana Chutney also contains tamarind.

Cumin seeds, a very pungent spice, are used to garnish many traditional Indian dishes. To dry-roast cumin seeds, place the seeds in a non-stick frying pan (skillet) and stir-fry over medium heat until a strong aroma rises. By far the best way to grind spices is in a coffee grinder kept especially for this purpose.

Lamb Curry with Cracked Wheat

Metric/Imperial
250 g/8 oz cracked wheat
Lamb Curry:
25 g/1 oz butter or ghee
  (page 8)
250 g/8 oz onions, chopped
3 × 2.5 cm/1 inch sticks
  cinnamon
10 cloves
10 small green cardamoms
4 large cardamoms
2 bay leaves
1 kg/2 lb lean lamb, cubed
50 g/2 oz fresh root ginger,
  peeled and finely grated
7-8 cloves garlic, peeled
  and crushed
2 teaspoons ground cumin

American
½ lb cracked wheat
Lamb Curry:
2 tablespoons butter or ghee
  (page 8)
½ lb onions, chopped
3 × 1 inch sticks cinnamon
10 cloves
10 small green cardamoms
4 large cardamoms
2 bay leaves
2 lb lean lamb, cubed
2 oz fresh gingerroot, peeled
  and finely grated
7-8 cloves garlic, peeled
  and crushed
2 teaspoons ground cumin
1 teaspoon chili powder

1 teaspoon chilli powder
1 teaspoon ground turmeric
150 ml/¼ pint natural
  yogurt
1.2 litres/2 pints water
To Serve:
125 g/4 oz butter, melted
freshly ground black pepper
25 g/1 oz fresh root ginger,
  peeled and finely chopped
2 green chillis, seeded and
  very finely chopped
3-4 sprigs coriander leaves,
  chopped
2 lemons, cut into wedges
500 g/1 lb onions, sliced
  and crisply fried

1 teaspoon ground turmeric
⅔ cup unflavored yogurt
5 cups water
To Serve:
½ cup butter, melted
freshly ground black pepper
1 oz fresh gingerroot, peeled
  and finely chopped
2 green chilis, seeded and
  very finely chopped
3-4 sprigs coriander leaves,
  chopped
2 lemons, cut into wedges
1 lb onions, sliced and
  crisply fried

1. Wash the wheat in cold water, then drain. Put in a bowl, cover with fresh cold water and soak overnight.
2. Drain the wheat and put in a saucepan with water to cover. Cook for 40 to 55 minutes or until the

wheat is soft, and has the consistency of porridge, stirring occasionally to prevent sticking.

3. To make the curry, heat the butter or ghee in a large, saucepan and sauté the onion until golden. Add the cinnamon sticks, cloves, cardamoms and bay leaves, and continue to sauté for 15 to 20 seconds. Add the meat, ginger, garlic, cumin, chilli powder, turmeric and yogurt. Mix well, cover and cook gently for about 20 to 30 minutes until nearly dry.

4. Increase the heat and sauté, stirring, for 1 to 2 minutes, then add the water. Cover and simmer for about 20 minutes until the meat is tender. Add the cooked wheat to the mixture, cover and cook for 40 to 50 minutes over gentle heat, stirring frequently. Add extra water if the mixture is too thick.

5. To serve, pour over the melted butter and grind the pepper on top. Garnish with the ginger, chilli, coriander, lemon wedges and onions. ·4·

Sour-sweet Chick Peas

Metric/Imperial
250 g/8 oz chick peas
1 teaspoon bicarbonate of soda
40 g/1½ oz tamarind pods
2 teaspoons brown sugar
250 g/8 oz potatoes, boiled, peeled and quartered
2 sprigs coriander leaves
1-2 green chillis, seeded and very finely chopped
1 medium onion, chopped
freshly ground black pepper
To Garnish:
15 g/½ oz cumin seeds, dry-roasted and ground (see introduction)

American
generous 1 cup chick peas
1 teaspoon baking soda
1½ oz tamarind pods
2 teaspoons brown sugar
½ lb potatoes, boiled, peeled and quartered
2 sprigs coriander leaves
1-2 green chilis, seeded and very finely chopped
1 medium onion, chopped
freshly ground black pepper
To Garnish:
1 tablespoon cumin seeds, dry-roasted and ground (see introduction)

Lamb curry with cracked wheat; Sour-sweet chick peas

1. Wash the chick peas in cold water. Place them in a bowl and cover with cold water to which the bicarbonate of soda (baking soda) has been added. Soak overnight.

2. Place the chick peas and their soaking liquid in a saucepan. Add enough fresh water to cover and cook for 1 to 1½ hours or until soft in the centre; drain.

3. Meanwhile, soak the tamarind pods in 350 ml/12 fl oz (1½ cups) hot water for 10 to 15 minutes and extract the pulpy liquid (see introduction). Repeat to extract any remaining pulp. Stir the brown sugar into the tamarind pulp and set aside.

4. Mix together the chick peas, potatoes, coriander, chillis, onion, and pepper to taste. Pour the tamarind mixture on top and stir well. Scatter over the ground cumin seeds and serve. ·4·

Spicy Turnips

Metric/Imperial
750 g/1½ lb turnips, peeled and sliced into rounds
75 g/3 oz ghee (page 8) or 125 g/4 oz butter
1 medium onion, sliced
1 green chilli, seeded and very finely chopped
1 teaspoon garam masala (page 37)
about ¼ teaspoon sugar (optional)
juice of 1 lemon

American
1½ lb turnips, peeled and sliced into rounds
⅓ cup ghee (page 8) or ½ cup butter
1 medium onion, sliced
1 green chili, seeded and very finely chopped
1 teaspoon garam masala (page 37)
about ¼ teaspoon sugar (optional)
juice of 1 lemon

1. Put the turnips and 85 ml/3 fl oz (6 tablespoons) water in a saucepan and simmer until tender and dry.

2. Heat the ghee or butter in another saucepan and sauté the onion until light brown. Add the chilli, turnips and garam masala. Cook for about 5 minutes. Taste and add the sugar, if liked. Sprinkle with lemon juice and serve. ·4·

Aubergine and Potatoes

Metric/Imperial	American
4 tablespoons oil	1/4 cup oil
2 onions, chopped	2 onions, chopped
1 aubergine, diced	1 eggplant, diced
3 medium potatoes, diced	3 medium potatoes, diced
1/2 teaspoon ground ginger	1/2 teaspoon ground ginger
1/2 teaspoon ground turmeric	1/2 teaspoon ground turmeric
1/4 teaspoon chilli powder	1/4 teaspoon chili powder
1/4 teaspoon garam masala (page 37)	1/4 teaspoon garam masala (page 37)
pinch of cayenne	pinch of cayenne
3 tomatoes, peeled and chopped	3 tomatoes, peeled and chopped
300 ml/1/2 pint water	1 1/4 cups water

1. Heat the oil in a saucepan and sauté the onions until golden brown. Add the aubergine (eggplant), potatoes and the spices. Stir and continue to sauté until the spices turn brown.
2. Add the tomatoes and water. Cover and cook gently for about 20 minutes, stirring frequently, until the vegetables are cooked and the liquid has been absorbed. ·14·

Banana Chutney

Metric/Imperial	American
75 g/3 oz tamarind pods	3 oz tamarind pods
2 tablespoons sugar	2 tablespoons sugar
50 g/2 oz raisins	1/3 cup raisins
50 g/2 oz sultanas	1/3 cup golden raisins
1 teaspoon chilli powder	1 teaspoon chili powder
15 g/1/2 oz fresh root ginger, peeled and grated	1/2 oz fresh gingerroot, peeled and grated
2 ripe bananas, peeled and sliced	2 ripe bananas, peeled and sliced
1 teaspoon cumin seeds, dry-roasted and ground (page 9)	1 teaspoon cumin seeds, dry-roasted and ground (page 9)

1. Soak the tamarind pods in 750 ml/1 1/4 pints (3 cups) hot water for 10 to 15 minutes and extract the pulpy liquid (see introduction). Repeat this process to extract any remaining pulp.
2. In a bowl, mix together the tamarind pulp, sugar, raisins, sultanas (golden raisins) and chilli powder. Stir to dissolve the sugar. Add the ginger.
3. Mix in the bananas. Sprinkle the chutney with the cumin. ·6·

C · O · U · N · T · D · O · W · N

Two days before:
Wash the cracked wheat, drain, cover with fresh cold water and leave to soak overnight.

The day before:
Prepare and cook the lamb curry with cracked wheat to the end of stage 4. Cool, cover and refrigerate. Wash the chick peas, then soak overnight.

On the day:
Prepare the sour-sweet chick peas without the garnish. Cover, cool and refrigerate. Prepare the spicy turnips, without the lemon juice. Make up the aubergine (eggplant) and potatoes. Make the banana chutney. Cover them and refrigerate.

To serve at 8 pm:
6.30: Remove the chutney from the refrigerator. Skim off any fat from the top of the lamb curry.
7.30: Reheat the lamb curry, pour over the melted butter and garnish.
7.40: Reheat the chick peas. Sprinkle with the cumin. Reheat the turnips and sprinkle with lemon juice. Reheat the aubergines and potatoes.
8.00: Take the dishes to the table.

F · R · E · E · Z · E · R · N · O · T · E · S

Prepare the lamb curry to the end of stage 4. Cool quickly. Skim off any fat from the top and pack into a foil container. Cover, seal and freeze for up to 2 months. To serve, thaw overnight in the refrigerator. Reheat gently in a saucepan, and garnish with ginger, chilli, coriander, lemon wedges and onions. ·4·

⸙M·E·N·U⸙

· 3 ·

Informal Supper for 4

Seekh Kebabs
Pork Vindaloo
Pea Pilau
Okra
Potato Raita

This meal may be eaten in the Western style – by serving different courses. Serve the kebabs as a first course with *naan* (page 63), or with either wholemeal (wholewheat) pitta or Arab bread, and a variety of chutneys. Use the recipe for banana chutney (page 12), apricot chutney (page 28), and mango chutney (page 32).

Not much pork is eaten in India, but the pork vindaloo recipe comes from Goa where the Catholic community – Goa was once a Portuguese colony – do eat a lot of pork. Goan food is pungent and it is usual to add at least 20 red chillis to a curry, which gives the dish its gorgeous red colour and fiery flavour. In this recipe the number has been drastically reduced and tomatoes included for colour. Serve the vindaloo with the pea pilau, okra and potato raita.

Using Basmati Rice

The most suitable rice, particularly for pilaus, is *basmati* – delicately aromatic, it cooks perfectly and quickly. First wash the rice – this is essential to get rid of excess starch. Place it in a bowl under cold running water. Swirl the rice around with your hand, then pour away the cloudy water.

Repeat this process five or six times, then leave to soak for 30 minutes. Drain the rice and use as directed.

Seekh Kebabs

Metric/Imperial	American
1 green chilli, seeded and very finely chopped	1 green chili, seeded and very finely chopped
15 g/½ oz fresh root ginger, peeled	½ oz fresh gingerroot, peeled
4 cloves garlic, peeled	4 cloves garlic, peeled
2 sprigs coriander leaves, finely chopped	2 sprigs coriander leaves, finely chopped
1 teaspoon cumin seeds	1 teaspoon cumin seeds
10 peppercorns	10 peppercorns
6 cloves	6 cloves
6 small cardamoms	6 small cardamoms
500 g/1 lb lean minced beef or lamb	1 lb lean ground beef or lamb
1 small onion, very finely chopped	1 small onion, very finely chopped
½ teaspoon chilli powder	½ teaspoon chili powder
1 egg, beaten	1 egg, beaten
a little oil	a little oil
1 lemon, sliced	1 lemon, sliced

1. Purée the green chilli, ginger, garlic, coriander leaves, cumin, peppercorns, cloves and cardamoms in a blender or food processor, adding a little water if necessary, to make a smooth paste.
2. Mix the meat and onion together, stir in the spice paste and chilli powder. Mix in enough beaten egg to make a firm consistency. Set aside for 2 to 3 minutes.
3. Divide the meat mixture into 12 portions. Rub a skewer with a little oil. Shape one portion of the mixture around the skewer to a length of about 10 cm/4 inches. Repeat with other skewers.
4. Place the kebabs on a grill (broiler) rack and cook under a preheated grill for 2 to 3 minutes on each side, brushing with a little oil, if necessary, when turned. Or, arrange the kebabs on a wire rack in a baking tray and cook in a preheated oven (190°C/375°F), Gas Mark 5, for 15 to 20 minutes, turning to cook evenly. Serve with lemon slices. ·11·

Pork Vindaloo

Metric/Imperial	American
120 ml/4 fl oz vinegar	½ cup vinegar
750 g/1½ lb lean pork, cubed	1½ lb lean pork, cubed
1 large onion, chopped	1 large onion, chopped
1 teaspoon cumin seeds	1 teaspoon cumin seeds
2 teaspoons mustard seeds	2 teaspoons mustard seeds
6 cloves garlic, peeled	6 cloves garlic, peeled
15 g/½ oz fresh root ginger, peeled	½ oz fresh gingerroot, peeled
2-4 small dried red chillis	2-4 small dried red chilis
4 cloves	4 cloves
1 × 2.5 cm/1 inch stick cinnamon	1 × 1 inch stick cinnamon
8 peppercorns	8 peppercorns
40 g/1½ oz ghee (page 8) or 3 tablespoons oil	3 tablespoons ghee (page 8) or oil
8 curry leaves	8 curry leaves
500 g/1 lb tomatoes, peeled and chopped	1 lb tomatoes, peeled and chopped
½ teaspoon ground turmeric	½ teaspoon ground turmeric

1. Blend 1 tablespoon of the vinegar with a little water and rinse the pork in this mixture. Drain and pat dry with absorbent kitchen paper.
2. Put the onion, cumin seeds, mustard seeds, garlic, ginger, chillis, cloves, cinnamon and peppercorns with a little of the remaining vinegar in a blender or food processor and work to a thick paste.
3. In a large bowl or dish, mix the pork cubes with this paste. Cover and set aside for 20 minutes.
4. Heat the ghee or oil in a large saucepan and sauté the curry leaves until golden. Add the pork, tomatoes and turmeric, stirring, until the tomatoes are broken down. Add remaining vinegar to taste.
5. Cover and simmer for 40 to 50 minutes or until the pork is tender. A little water may be added during cooking if necessary, although the sauce should be fairly thick. Serve immediately.

Pea Pilau

Metric/Imperial
500 g/1 lb basmati rice
75 g/3 oz ghee (page 8) or
  butter
2 onions, sliced into rings
pinch of ground cloves
1 teaspoon ground
  cinnamon or small stick
  of cinnamon
5 bay leaves
250 g/8 oz peas, shelled
1.2 litres/2 pints vegetable
  stock or water
salt
freshly ground black pepper
¼ teaspoon chilli powder

American
2⅔ cups basmati rice
⅓ cup ghee (page 8) or
  butter
2 onions, sliced into rings
pinch of ground cloves
1 teaspoon ground
  cinnamon or small stick
  of cinnamon
5 bay leaves
1½ cups shelled peas
5 cups vegetable stock or
  water
salt
freshly ground black pepper
¼ teaspoon chili powder

1. Wash the rice and soak in cold water for 30 minutes, then drain thoroughly (see introduction).
2. Heat the ghee or butter in a large pan and sauté the onion rings until golden brown. Add the cloves, cinnamon and bay leaves. Cook, stirring, for 1 minute.
3. Stir in the rice and cook until the grains are transparent. Add the peas and continue cooking, stirring, for 1 minute. Pour in the stock or water. Add salt and pepper to taste and the chilli powder.
4. Bring to the boil, cover and simmer until the rice and peas are cooked and the liquid is absorbed. If preferred, the cooking can be done in a preheated oven (170°C/325°F), Gas Mark 3. Dry the rice, uncovered, in the oven until the grains are separate.

Seekh kebabs to serve as a starter with Naan bread (page 63); Pork vindaloo

Okra

Metric/Imperial	American
50 g/2 oz ghee (page 8) or butter	¼ cup ghee (page 8) or butter
1 large onion, sliced	1 large onion, sliced
3 cloves garlic, peeled and sliced	3 cloves garlic, peeled and sliced
1 × 2.5 cm/1 inch piece fresh root ginger, peeled and finely chopped	1 × 1 inch piece fresh gingerroot, peeled and finely chopped
2 green chillis, seeded and finely chopped	2 green chilis, seeded and finely chopped
½ teaspoon chilli powder	½ teaspoon chili powder
500 g/1 lb okra, topped and tailed	1 lb okra, trimmed
200 ml/⅓ pint water	⅞ cup water
salt	salt
2 teaspoons desiccated coconut	2 teaspoons shredded coconut

1. Melt the ghee or butter in a heavy saucepan and gently sauté the onion, garlic, ginger, chillis and chilli powder for 5 minutes, stirring, until soft.
2. Add the okra, water and salt to taste. Bring to the boil, then lower the heat, cover and simmer for 5 to 10 minutes until the okra are just tender, but still firm to the bite. Stir in the coconut and serve hot. ·4·

Potato Raita

Metric/Imperial	American
250 g/8 oz potatoes, peeled	½ lb potatoes, peeled
salt	salt
750 ml/1¼ pints natural yogurt	3 cups unflavored yogurt
1 teaspoon cumin seeds	1 teaspoon cumin seeds
¼ teaspoon chilli powder	¼ teaspoon chili powder
freshly ground black pepper	freshly ground black pepper
chopped coriander leaves, to garnish	chopped coriander leaves, to garnish

1. Cook the potatoes in a saucepan of boiling salted water until just tender. Drain and cool, then dice.
2. Mix the yogurt in a bowl with the cumin seeds, chilli powder and salt and pepper to taste. Chill.
3. Mix the potatoes into the yogurt just before serving. Garnish the Potato Raita with chopped coriander leaves.

C · O · U · N · T · D · O · W · N

The day before:
Prepare the kebab mixture. Cover with cling film (plastic wrap) and refrigerate. Prepare the pork vindaloo. Cool, cover and refrigerate.

On the day:
Wash and soak the rice. Prepare the pea pilau and, when cooked, transfer to an ovenproof serving dish. Cover tightly with foil and a lid. Prepare and cook the potatoes for the potato raita, then set aside to cool. Keep covered. Mix the yogurt with the spices, put into a serving bowl, cover and refrigerate.

To serve at 8 pm:
7.00: Remove the vindaloo from the refrigerator and skim off any fat from the top. Shape the kebabs on the skewers. Prepare and cook the okra.
7.10: Preheat the oven to 180°C/350°F, Gas Mark 4.
7.30: Reheat the pilau in the oven. Add the potatoes to the yogurt and garnish the dish with chopped fresh coriander leaves.
7.40: Reheat the vindaloo.
7.45: Preheat the grill (broiler) to very hot. Put the kebabs to cook.
8.00: Garnish the vindaloo. Serve the kebabs.

F · R · E · E · Z · E · R · N · O · T · E · S

The prepared mixture for the kebabs can be packed in a polythene (plastic) bag, sealed and frozen for up to 2 months. To serve, thaw at room temperature for 4 hours or more, and cook as directed. Cook the vindaloo, then cool quickly. Skim off any fat from the top, store in a rigid container and freeze for up to 6 weeks. Heat gently to serve.

⠿M⬩E⬩N⬩U⠿

· 4 ·

Sunday Lunch for 4

Chicken Curry
Dhal
Vegetable Pilau
Courgettes with Potatoes
Raita with Tiny Pakoras

The Standby of the Raj

Chicken curry was the great standby in the days of the Raj. It was (and still is) often on the menu, especially for Sunday luncheon, in railway station restaurants, the army officers' mess and club dining rooms. The chickens may have been tough – they spent a lifetime scratching in the dust and laying eggs before being brought to an abrupt end – but they were tasty. And so were the curries.

The recipe given here is a simple one using tomatoes to provide colour. If you prefer a smoother texture, with a stronger flavour and colour, use tomato juice instead of the canned tomatoes. If the sauce becomes too thick, dilute it with a little water.

Favourite Accompaniments

Dhal is the Indian name for all members of the legume or pulse family, of which the red lentil is one of the commonest. Dhal is an inexpensive source of protein and plays an important part in the Indian diet. In one form or another – there are more than 50 varieties in India alone – dhal is served at every meal.

Raita is *the* accompaniment for a spicy meal. It has a cooling effect and sets off the more aromatic dishes. Mixing tiny fritter-like pakoras into the raita is the traditional way to serve it.

Chicken Curry

Metric/Imperial

3 tablespoons oil
1 onion, sliced
1 cinnamon stick
4 small green cardamoms
*2 green chillis, halved and
    seeded*
*50 g/2 oz fresh root ginger,
    peeled and finely sliced*
*6-7 cloves garlic, peeled
    and finely sliced*
8 chicken portions, skinned
2 teaspoons ground cumin
*3-4 sprigs coriander leaves,
    chopped*
*1 × 397 g/14 oz can
    tomatoes*

American

3 tablespoons oil
1 onion, sliced
1 cinnamon stick
4 small green cardamoms
*2 green chilis, halved and
    seeded*
*2 oz fresh gingerroot, peeled
    and finely sliced*
*6-7 cloves garlic, peeled
    and finely sliced*
8 chicken portions, skinned
2 teaspoons ground cumin
*3-4 sprigs coriander leaves,
    chopped*
1 × 14 oz can tomatoes

Chicken curry

1. Heat the ghee or oil in a very large saucepan and sauté the onion until light brown. Add the cinnamon, cardamoms and chillis and sauté for 1 minute. Stir in the ginger and garlic and sauté for 30 seconds. Add the chicken portions and sauté for a further 10 to 15 minutes.

2. Add the cumin and coriander leaves and sauté for 1 to 2 minutes, then stir in the tomatoes. Cover and simmer over gentle heat for 30 to 35 minutes or until the chicken is tender. ·2·

Dhal

Metric/Imperial

*250 g/8 oz red lentils,
    thoroughly washed*
450 ml/¾ pint water
½ teaspoon ground turmeric
*2 teaspoons ground
    coriander or 3 sprigs
    coriander leaves, chopped*

American

*1 cup red lentils,
    thoroughly washed*
2 cups water
½ teaspoon ground turmeric
*2 teaspoons ground
    coriander or 3 sprigs
    coriander leaves, chopped*

salt
6 curry leaves (optional)
50 g/2 oz butter
1 small onion, chopped

salt
6 curry leaves (optional)
1/4 cup butter
1 small onion, chopped

1. Put the lentils, water, turmeric and coriander in a saucepan and simmer for 15 to 20 minutes.
2. Using a potato masher, mash the lentil mixture. Stir in the salt and curry leaves, if using. Cover and simmer gently for about 20 to 30 minutes. Remove from the heat and set aside.
3. Melt the butter in a small frying pan (skillet) and sauté the onion until light brown. Tip the onion and butter into the dhal and serve. ·2·

Vegetable Pilau

Metric/Imperial	American
350 g/12 oz basmati rice	*1 3/4 cups basmati rice*
salt	*salt*
4 tablespoons ghee (page 8)	*4 tablespoons ghee (page 8)*
or oil	*or oil*
10 whole cardamoms	*10 whole cardamoms*
10 cloves	*10 cloves*
2 cinnamon sticks	*2 cinnamon sticks*
2 onions, sliced	*2 onions, sliced*
3 cloves garlic, peeled and	*3 cloves garlic, peeled and*
finely chopped	*finely chopped*
1 × 2.5 cm/1 inch piece	*1 × 1 inch piece fresh*
fresh root ginger, peeled	*gingerroot, peeled and*
and grated	*grated*
750 g/1 1/2 lb mixed	*1 1/2 lb mixed vegetables*
vegetables (carrots,	*(carrots, zucchini, peas,*
courgettes, peas,	*eggplant, potatoes), cut*
aubergine, potatoes), cut	*in pieces*
in pieces	*1 × 14 oz can chopped*
1 × 397 g/14 oz can	*tomatoes*
chopped tomatoes	*1/2 teaspoon chili powder*
1/2 teaspoon chilli powder	*few sprigs coriander leaves,*
few sprigs coriander leaves,	*to garnish*
to garnish	

1. Wash the rice and soak in cold water for 30 minutes, then drain thoroughly.
2. Bring a large saucepan of salted water to the boil. Add the rice and boil for 3 minutes. Drain and set aside.
3. Heat 3 tablespoons of the ghee or oil in the rinsed out pan and sauté the cardamom, cloves and cinnamon for a few seconds. Add the onions, garlic and ginger and sauté, stirring, for 5 minutes.
4. Put in the vegetables and stir-fry for 1 to 2 minutes. Pour in the tomatoes and add the chilli powder and salt to taste. Cover and simmer gently for about 15 minutes or until the vegetables are tender.
5. Grease a casserole dish with the remaining ghee or oil. Layer the vegetables and rice in the dish, ending with a layer of vegetables. Cover the casserole tightly with foil and then with the lid. Cook in a preheated oven (180°C/350°F), Gas Mark 4, for 30 minutes or until the rice is cooked. Garnish with the coriander leaves and serve.

Courgettes with Potatoes

Metric/Imperial	American
25 g/1 oz ghee (page 8) or	*2 tablespoons ghee (page 8)*
2 tablespoons oil	*or oil*
1 teaspoon cumin seeds	*1 teaspoon cumin seeds*
pinch of asafetida (page	*pinch of asafetida (page*
49) (optional)	*49) (optional)*
2 potatoes, peeled and cubed	*2 potatoes, peeled and cubed*
500 g/1 lb courgettes, sliced	*1 lb zucchini, sliced*
about 1/2 teaspoon chilli	*about 1/2 teaspoon chili*
powder	*powder*
1/2 teaspoon ground turmeric	*1/2 teaspoon ground turmeric*
1 teaspoon ground coriander	*1 teaspoon ground coriander*
salt	*salt*
1 teaspoon garam masala	*1 teaspoon garam masala*
(page 37)	*(page 37)*
chopped coriander leaves, to	*chopped coriander leaves, to*
garnish	*garnish*

1. Heat the ghee or oil in a large saucepan and sauté the cumin seeds and asafetida, if using, until the seeds crackle. Add the potatoes and sauté for 10 minutes. Stir in the courgettes (zucchini), chilli powder, turmeric, coriander and salt to taste.

2. Cover and cook gently for 15 minutes or until the potatoes are tender. Sprinkle on the garam masala and garnish with chopped coriander leaves. ·9·

Raita with Tiny Pakoras

Metric/Imperial	American
50 g/2 oz chick pea flour (besan)	½ cup chick pea flour (besan)
pinch of baking powder	pinch of baking powder
4-5 tablespoons water	4-5 tablespoons water
oil, for deep-frying	oil, for deep-frying
Raita:	Raita:
300 ml/½ pint natural yogurt	1¼ cups unflavored yogurt
salt	salt
freshly ground black pepper	freshly ground black pepper
1 teaspoon cumin seeds, dry roasted and coarsely ground (page 9)	1 teaspoon cumin seeds, dry-roasted and coarsely ground (page 9)
To Garnish:	To Garnish:
1 green chilli, seeded and very finely chopped	1 green chili, seeded and very finely chopped
1-2 sprigs coriander leaves, chopped	1-2 sprigs coriander leaves, chopped

1. Sift the flour and baking powder into a bowl. Gradually beat in enough water to make a thick batter.

2. Heat the oil in a deep-fryer to 190°C/375°F or until a cube of bread browns in 30 seconds. Hold a perforated ladle over the hot oil. Pour a little of the batter into the ladle. Quickly shake the ladle so that small drops of the batter fall into the oil. Fry for 3 to 4 minutes until crisp. Drain on absorbent kitchen paper.

3. Beat the yogurt and salt and pepper to taste in a bowl. Stir in the tiny pakoras. Sprinkle with the cumin, and garnish with chopped chilli and coriander leaves. Chill before serving.

Cook's Tip:
Pakoras are sometimes called *boondi* and can be bought ready-made from Asian shops but, of course, are better when homemade.

C · O · U · N · T · D · O · W · N
The day before:
Make the chicken curry and the dhal (but do not add the onion). Cool, cover and refrigerate.

On the day:
Make the vegetable pilau and transfer to an oven-proof serving dish. Cover tightly with foil and lid. Prepare the courgettes (zucchini) and potatoes, cover with cold water. Prepare and deep-fry the pakoras for the raita. Beat the yogurt and mix in the pakoras. Cover and refrigerate.

To serve at 8 pm:
7.00: Remove the curry from the refrigerator and skim off any fat from the top. Make the courgettes with potatoes. Keep hot.
7.10: Preheat the oven to 180°C/350°F, Gas Mark 4.
7.30: Reheat the chicken curry and dhal.
7.45: Sauté the onion and add to the dhal.
8.00: Add any garnishes and serve.

F · R · E · E · Z · E · R · N · O · T · E · S
Make the chicken curry. Cool quickly, skim off any fat from the top and place in a rigid container. Cover, seal and freeze for up to 2 months. To serve, thaw overnight in the refrigerator and heat gently on top of the cooker, or in a preheated oven (180°C/350°F), Gas Mark 4, until piping hot. Make the dhal, but do not add the sautéed onion. Cool quickly and put in a rigid container. Cover, seal and freeze for up to 6 months. To serve, thaw at room temperature for 3 to 4 hours. Heat gently until very hot. Sauté the onions and add to the dhal.

⁖M·E·N·U⁖

· 5 ·

Hot Fork Supper for 4

Parsee-style Fish
Lamb with Spinach
Kitcheri
Aubergine Bhartha
Potatoes and Peas

The Parsee-style fish is a chilli-flavoured dish that comes from Bombay on the west coast of India. Parsee cuisine is distinctive in its use of ingredients. This recipe cleverly uses eggs and vinegar to create a delicious sauce for fish. Pomfret is the traditional choice of fish for this but sole or plaice make excellent alternatives. Serve as a first course with crusty French bread.

The lamb with spinach, a north Indian dish, is usually made with goat or kid, because Hindus, the majority community in India, have a religious taboo against eating beef. However, beef can be used – choose chuck or any good quality stewing steak. If using beef, you will need to increase the cooking time. This lamb dish is served with the vegetable recipes and the *kitcheri*. If you prefer, leave out the rice and serve with Indian bread instead, like *chapatis* or *parathas* (pages 62 and 63).

Kitcheri was known and appreciated by the British and other European colonists in the seventeenth century. Later it was transformed into the popular 'kedgeree' we know today by replacing the lentils with fish.

Versatile Aubergine

Bhartha is a classic dish of puréed aubergine (eggplant). In India the aubergine is roasted in hot ashes, which gives the dish its characteristic smoky flavour. In this recipe the aubergine is softened in the oven.

Parsee-style Fish

Metric/Imperial	American
500 g/1 lb white fish, filleted	1 lb white fish, filleted
3 cloves garlic, peeled and crushed	3 cloves garlic, peeled and crushed
1 teaspoon ground cumin	1 teaspoon ground cumin
1/2 teaspoon chilli powder	1/2 teaspoon chili powder
2 tablespoons oil	2 tablespoons oil
2 onions, sliced	2 onions, sliced
3 chillis	3 chilis
450 ml/3/4 pint water	2 cups water
salt	salt
3/4 tablespoon cornflour	3/4 tablespoon cornstarch
1 egg	1 egg
4 tablespoons vinegar	1/4 cup vinegar
sugar	sugar
To Garnish:	To Garnish:
lemon wedges	lemon wedges
chopped coriander leaves	chopped coriander leaves
pilau rice, to serve (page 51)	pilau rice, to serve (page 51)

1. Cut the fish into 8 pieces. Mix the garlic to a paste with the cumin and chilli powder.
2. Heat the oil in a large saucepan and sauté the onions until golden brown. Add the whole chillis and garlic and spice paste. Continue to sauté for about 1 minute until the spices darken.
3. Pour in the water and simmer for 5 minutes. Add salt to taste. Mix the cornflour (cornstarch) to a smooth paste with a little cold water, then stir into the sauce.
4. Add the fish pieces to the pan and simmer for 5 to 10 minutes or until the fish is tender, stirring gently.
5. Beat the egg with the vinegar and stir into the sauce. Add sugar to taste and simmer for 3 minutes. Transfer to a warm serving dish. Garnish with lemon and coriander; and serve with pilau rice. ·14·

Lamb with Spinach

Metric/Imperial	American
1 kg/2 lb fresh spinach, washed thoroughly and chopped, or 2 × 225 g/ 8 oz frozen leaf spinach, thawed and chopped	2 lb fresh spinach, washed thoroughly and chopped, or 2 × 8 oz packets frozen leaf spinach, thawed and chopped
50 g/2 oz ghee (page 8) or 4 tablespoons oil	4 tablespoons ghee (page 8) or oil
1 small onion, sliced	1 small onion, sliced
40 g/1 1/2 oz fresh root ginger, peeled and crushed	1 1/2 oz fresh gingerroot, peeled and crushed
5 cloves garlic, crushed	5 cloves garlic, crushed
1 teaspoon chilli powder	1 teaspoon chili powder
1 teaspoon ground coriander	1 teaspoon ground coriander
1 teaspoon ground cumin	1 teaspoon ground cumin
4 tomatoes, peeled and roughly chopped	4 tomatoes, peeled and roughly chopped
1/2 teaspoon ground turmeric	1/2 teaspoon ground turmeric
750 g/1 1/2 lb boned leg or shoulder of lamb, cut into small cubes	1 1/2 lb boned leg or shoulder of lamb, cut into small cubes
200 ml/1/3 pint water	1 cup water

1. If using fresh spinach, place in a saucepan with the water that clings to the leaves and cook for 10 minutes, then strain. Either sieve or blend the fresh or frozen spinach to make a purée and set aside.
2. Heat the ghee or oil in a large saucepan and sauté the onion until light brown. Add the ginger, garlic, chilli powder, coriander and cumin and sauté gently for 1 to 2 minutes. Add the tomatoes and turmeric. Continue to sauté gently for 10 to 15 minutes until the ghee or oil separates and rises to the surface. Add the meat and cook for 7 minutes or until dry.
3. Add the water, cover and cook gently for 30 to 40 minutes. After 15 minutes, when the sauce has been reduced by half, add the spinach purée. Stir well, cover and simmer for the remaining time. ·9·

Lamb with spinach

1. Wash the rice and lentils thoroughly. Put in a bowl and cover with cold water. Leave to soak for 2 hours.
2. Melt the ghee in a heavy saucepan and gently sauté the onion and garlic until soft. Add the turmeric, cloves, cardamoms, cinnamon and pepper to taste and sauté for a further 3 minutes, stirring constantly.
3. Drain the rice and lentils, add to the pan and toss for 5 minutes until every grain is coated. Add the water and bring to the boil. Lower the heat, cover with a tight-fitting lid and simmer for 20 to 30 minutes until the rice and lentils are cooked.
4. Remove the lid and boil off any excess liquid before serving, stirring to prevent sticking.

Kitcheri

Metric/Imperial	American
350 g/12 oz long-grain rice	1½ cups long-grain rice
175 g/6 oz lentils	¾ cup lentils
125 g/4 oz ghee (page 8) or butter	½ cup ghee (page 8) or butter
1 large onion, sliced	1 large onion, sliced
2 cloves garlic, peeled and sliced	2 cloves garlic, peeled and sliced
1 teaspoon ground turmeric	1 teaspoon ground turmeric
10 whole cloves	10 whole cloves
6 whole cardamoms	6 whole cardamoms
1 × 7.5 cm/3 inch cinnamon stick	1 × 3 inch cinnamon stick
1 teaspoon freshly ground black pepper	1 teaspoon freshly ground black pepper
900 ml/1½ pints boiling water	4 cups boiling water

Aubergine Bhartha

Metric/Imperial	American
1 kg/2 lb aubergines	2 lb eggplants
about 6 tablespoons oil	about ½ cup oil
1 green chilli, seeded	1 green chili, seeded
10 peppercorns	10 peppercorns
2 cloves garlic, peeled	2 cloves garlic, peeled
½ teaspoon ground turmeric	½ teaspoon ground turmeric
3 onions, chopped	3 onions, chopped
1 × 2.5 cm/1 inch piece fresh root ginger, peeled and chopped	1 × 1 inch piece fresh gingerroot, peeled and chopped
4 tomatoes, peeled and mashed	4 tomatoes, peeled and mashed
¼ teaspoon chilli powder	¼ teaspoon chili powder
salt	salt
freshly ground black pepper	freshly ground black pepper
chopped coriander leaves, to garnish	chopped coriander leaves, to garnish

1. Brush the aubergines (eggplants) with a little of the oil. Bake in a preheated oven (180°C/350°F), Gas Mark 4, for about 45 minutes or until tender. When cool, remove the skins and mash the pulp.

2. Using an electric grinder or pestle and mortar, grind the chilli, peppercorns, garlic and turmeric together to form a paste.

3. Heat 5 tablespoons of the oil in a large frying pan (skillet) and sauté the onions until golden brown. Add the spice paste and ginger and cook, stirring, for 2 minutes.

4. Add the mashed aubergines and cook until slightly browned, stirring well. Mix in the tomatoes, chilli powder and salt and pepper to taste. Cover and cook gently over low heat for 15 minutes. Garnish with coriander leaves before serving.

Potatoes and Peas

Metric/Imperial	American
40 g/1½ oz ghee (page 8) or 3 tablespoons oil	3 tablespoons ghee (page 8) or oil
1½ teaspoons cumin seeds	1½ teaspoons cumin seeds
500 g/1 lb potatoes, peeled and diced	1 lb potatoes, peeled and diced
about 1 teaspoon chilli powder	about 1 teaspoon chili powder
½ teaspoon ground turmeric	½ teaspoon ground turmeric
1½ teaspoons ground coriander	1½ teaspoons ground coriander
1 × 225 g/8 oz can tomatoes	1 × 8 oz can tomatoes
salt	salt
125 g/4 oz shelled green peas	¼ lb shelled green peas
1 green pepper, seeded and sliced	1 green pepper, seeded and sliced
200 ml/⅓ pint water	1 cup water
chopped coriander leaves, to garnish	chopped coriander leaves, to garnish

1. Heat the ghee or oil in a large saucepan and sauté the cumin seeds until they crackle. Add the potatoes and sauté for 3 to 4 minutes. Stir in the chilli powder, turmeric and coriander, and continue to sauté for 1 to 2 minutes, stirring continuously.

2. Stir in the tomatoes, salt, peas and pepper. Cover and cook gently for 1 minute, then stir in the water. Cook until the potatoes are tender. Garnish with chopped coriander leaves. ·11·

C · O · U · N · T · D · O · W · N

The day before:
Prepare and cook the lamb with spinach and the aubergine bhartha. Cool, cover and refrigerate.

On the day:
Make the kitcheri and transfer to an ovenproof dish. Cover tightly with foil and a lid. Prepare the potatoes and cover with cold water.

To serve at 8 pm:
7.00: Make the potatoes and peas. Start preparing the fish.
7.05: Preheat the oven to 180°C/350°F, Gas Mark 4.
7.25: Reheat the kitcheri in the oven.
7.30: Gently reheat the lamb and the bhartha on top of the cooker. Cook the parsee-style fish.
7.50: Garnish the aubergine bhartha and the potatoes and peas.
7.55: Add the egg and vinegar to the fish and serve immediately.

F · R · E · E · Z · E · R · N · O · T · E · S

Cook the lamb with spinach. Cool quickly and skim off any fat from the top. Spoon into a rigid container, cover, seal and freeze for up to 2 months. To serve, thaw at room temperature for 4 hours, then simmer gently until piping hot. Prepare the aubergine bhartha. Cool quickly and spoon into a rigid container. Cover, seal and freeze for up to 3 months. Thaw before reheating over gentle heat or in a preheated oven (180°C/350°F), Gas Mark 4.

Variation:
Serve the main course with apricot or mango chutney (page 28 and 32) and a salad of chopped tomatoes and onions, dressed with lemon juice and garnished with chopped green chilli.

⸙M·E·N·U⸙

· 6 ·

Vegetarian Lunch for 4

Egg Curry
Spicy Prawn Rice
Curried Cauliflower
Cabbage and Potato
Apricot Chutney

Strictly Vegetarian

As there are a great number of vegetarians in India, because of religious beliefs, Indian cooking has always produced many non-meat meals; providing a welcome addition to the European vegetarians' diet.

Making a Substantial Meal

Obviously the vegetable and fish dishes can be extended. Dhals (page 18), rich in protein, are often included. A rice dish adds bulk and Indian bread can be served as well. To start the meal, one of the snacks or savouries on pages 5 to 8 would be ideal. For the finale, serve creamed rice (page 44), semolina halwa (page 52), a fresh fruit salad or other Indian sweetmeat.

The Convenience of Rice

If entertaining it may be more convenient to serve a rice dish instead of bread because it can be cooked in advance and reheated in the oven without any trouble. However, if you prefer to serve bread, the ubiquitous *chapati* (page 62), or *puri* (page 62) – easy to make and deep-fried – will go well with this meal. Tasty, fat-free and made with wholemeal flour, Arab or pitta bread is an easy option. Store in the freezer and warm it (no need to thaw) in a moderate oven at the last minute.

Egg Curry

Metric/Imperial	American
25 g/1 oz ghee (page 8) or 2 tablespoons oil	2 tablespoons ghee (page 8) or oil
2 medium onions, chopped	2 medium onions, chopped
1 × 2.5 cm/1 inch stick cinnamon	1 × 1 inch stick cinnamon
2 cloves garlic, peeled and crushed	2 cloves garlic, peeled and crushed
1 teaspoon grated fresh root ginger or ground ginger	1 teaspoon grated fresh gingerroot or ground ginger
about 1 teaspoon chilli powder	about 1 teaspoon chili powder
1 teaspoon ground cumin	1 teaspoon ground cumin
1 1/2 teaspoons ground coriander	1 1/2 teaspoons ground coriander
1 teaspoon garam masala (page 37)	1 teaspoon garam masala (page 37)
4 tomatoes, peeled and chopped, or 1 × 225 g/8 oz can tomatoes, chopped	4 tomatoes, peeled and chopped, or 1 × 8 oz can tomatoes, chopped
salt	salt
freshly ground black pepper	freshly ground black pepper
6-8 hard-boiled eggs, halved	6-8 hard-cooked eggs, halved
coriander or celery leaves, to garnish	coriander or celery leaves, to garnish

1. Heat the ghee or oil in a saucepan and gently sauté the onion. Add the cinnamon and stir for a few seconds. Stir in the garlic, ginger, chilli powder, cumin, coriander and garam masala, and continue cooking gently for 30 seconds.
2. Add the tomatoes and salt and pepper to taste; cook for 5 minutes until the sauce thickens slightly. Stir occasionally to prevent sticking.
3. Carefully add the eggs, cover and simmer gently for 8 to 10 minutes. Garnish with coriander or celery leaves. ·9·

Spicy Prawn Rice

Metric/Imperial	American
250 g/8 oz long-grain rice	1 1/4 cups long-grain rice
salt	salt
1 × 1 cm/1/2 inch piece fresh root ginger, peeled and very finely chopped	1 × 1/2 inch piece fresh gingerroot, peeled and very finely chopped
1 clove garlic, peeled and crushed	1 clove garlic, peeled and crushed
175 g/6 oz peeled prawns, thawed if frozen	1 cup shelled shrimp, thawed if frozen
1 teaspoon garam masala (page 37)	1 teaspoon garam masala (page 37)
1/2 teaspoon chilli powder	1/2 teaspoon chili powder
2 tablespoons lemon juice	2 tablespoons lemon juice
50 g/2 oz butter or ghee (page 8)	1/4 cup butter or ghee (page 8)
To Garnish:	To Garnish:
finely chopped fresh red chilli (optional)	finely chopped red chili (optional)
unpeeled prawns	unshelled shrimp

1. Cook the rice in a large saucepan of boiling salted water for 12 minutes, then drain.
2. Combine the ginger and garlic. Put the prawns (shrimp) in a bowl, add the ginger, garlic, garam masala, 1/2 teaspoon salt, the chilli powder and lemon juice. Stir well to mix and leave for 1 hour in a cool place.
3. Melt the butter or ghee in a large frying pan (skillet) with a lid, add the rice and fork through over a gentle heat for 3 to 4 minutes. Add the prawns with the marinating liquid and fork through. Cover and gently simmer for 5 minutes to allow all ingredients to heat through.
4. Taste and adjust the seasoning, transfer to a warm serving dish and garnish with chopped chilli and unpeeled prawns.

Cabbage and potato; Curried cauliflower

Curried Cauliflower

Metric/Imperial

1 medium cauliflower,
  broken into florets
50 g/2 oz ghee (page 8) or
  4 tablespoons oil
2 teaspoons cumin seeds
1 teaspoon chilli powder
1/2 teaspoon ground turmeric
2 teaspoons ground
  coriander
salt
2 teaspoons garam masala
  (page 37)
juice of 1 lemon
mint sprigs, to garnish

American

1 medium cauliflower,
  broken into flowerets
4 tablespoons ghee
  (page 8) or oil
2 teaspoons cumin seeds
1 teaspoon chili powder
1/2 teaspoon ground turmeric
2 teaspoons ground
  coriander
salt
2 teaspoons garam masala
  (page 37)
juice of 1 lemon
mint sprigs, to garnish

1. Cut the cauliflower florets into medium-sized pieces. Slice the remaining cauliflower stem after peeling away any tough skin. Discard the large leaves but retain a few of the tender smaller leaves. Wash in cold water and drain thoroughly.
2. Heat the ghee or oil in a saucepan and sauté the cumin seeds until they crackle. Add the cauliflower pieces and leaves; continue cooking for 6 minutes.
3. Stir in the chilli, turmeric, coriander, salt to taste, garam masala and lemon juice. Cover and cook gently for 10 to 15 minutes until the cauliflower is tender and the mixture is dry. If necessary, add a little water during cooking to prevent the mixture sticking. Garnish with mint sprigs. ·7·

Cabbage and Potato

Metric/Imperial

1/4 teaspoon fenugreek seeds
1 teaspoon cumin seeds
1/2 teaspoon aniseed
1/2 teaspoon mustard seeds
1/2 teaspoon onion seeds
25-40 g/1-1 1/2 oz ghee
  (page 8) or
  2-3 tablespoons oil
2 medium potatoes, peeled
  and cut into chunks
1 bay leaf
500 g/1 lb cabbage,
  chopped
1 teaspoon chilli powder
1/2 teaspoon ground turmeric
2 teaspoons ground
  coriander
1 teaspoon sugar
1/2 teaspoon ground
  cinnamon
1/2 teaspoon ground
  cardamom
1/2 teaspoon ground cloves

American

1/4 teaspoon fenugreek seeds
1 teaspoon cumin seeds
1/2 teaspoon aniseed
1/2 teaspoon mustard seeds
1/2 teaspoon onion seeds
2-3 tablespoons ghee
  (page 8) or oil
2 medium potatoes, peeled
  and cut into chunks
1 bay leaf
1 lb cabbage, chopped
1 teaspoon chili powder
1/2 teaspoon ground turmeric
2 teaspoons ground
  coriander
1 teaspoon sugar
1/2 teaspoon ground
  cinnamon
1/2 teaspoon ground
  cardamom
1/2 teaspoon ground cloves

1. Mix together the fenugreek, cumin, aniseed, mustard and onion seeds in a small bowl.
2. Heat the ghee or oil in a large saucepan and sauté the potatoes for 4 to 5 minutes. Add the mixture of seeds and the bay leaf, and sauté for a few seconds. Stir in the cabbage, chilli powder, turmeric, coriander and sugar. Cover and cook gently for 10 minutes.
3. Sprinkle the cinnamon, cardamom and cloves on to the cabbage and mix well. Cover and cook for a further 8 to 10 minutes or until the potatoes are tender. ·11·

Apricot Chutney

Metric/Imperial	American
250 g/8 oz dried apricots, soaked overnight	1/2 lb dried apricots, soaked overnight
150 ml/1/4 pint vinegar	2/3 cup vinegar
250 g/8 oz sugar	1 cup sugar
25 g/1 oz fresh root ginger, peeled and crushed	1 oz fresh gingerroot, peeled and crushed
4 cloves garlic, peeled and crushed	4 cloves garlic, peeled and crushed
1 teaspoon chilli powder	1 teaspoon chili powder
salt	salt

1. Place the apricots and the soaking liquid with enough water to cover in a saucepan. Simmer until tender, then beat or blend the mixture to a smooth consistency.
2. Place the vinegar, sugar, ginger, garlic, chilli powder and salt to taste in a separate pan. Heat gently, stirring, until the sugar has dissolved, then increase the heat until a syrup is formed.
3. Stir the apricots into the syrup and simmer gently for about 10 minutes until the desired thickness.
4. Allow the chutney to cool. Bottle in airtight jars with vinegar-proof tops. ·2·7·

Optional Extra:
Poppadoms are paper-thin savoury wafers made from chick pea flour (*besan*). They are served as an accompaniment to a meal but are excellent with drinks. Poppadoms are available plain or spiced with black pepper or chilli. Store them in an airtight container in a cool dry place. Poppadoms can be shallow fried or grilled (broiled). Before cooking, tap the poppadoms on the table to get rid of the dust. When shallow frying, heat the oil until really hot. Slip in a poppadom and press down with a fish slice or spatula. Turn over and fry the other side. Drain.

C·O·U·N·T·D·O·W·N
The week before:
Make the apricot chutney and store in a cool place.
The day before:
Make the curry sauce for the egg curry, but do not add the eggs. Cool, cover and refrigerate.
On the day:
If necessary, take the prawns (shrimp) out of the freezer and leave to thaw. When thawed, tip into a strainer; leave to drain. Prepare and cook the spicy prawn rice. Turn out into an ovenproof dish; cover tightly. Skim off any fat from the top of the curry sauce. Prepare the cauliflower, cabbage and potatoes. Cover the potatoes with cold water.
To serve at 1 pm:
11.00: Make the curried cauliflower and keep warm. Prepare the cabbage and potato and keep warm.
12.10: Preheat the oven to 180°C/350°F, Gas Mark 4. Hard-boil (hard-cook) the eggs and finish making the curry.
12.30: Reheat the spicy prawn rice in the oven.
12.55: Spoon the chutney into a serving bowl.
1.00: Garnish the curry and rice dishes. Take the dishes to the table.

F·R·E·E·Z·E·R · N·O·T·E·S
Make the curry sauce without the eggs. Cool quickly and skim off any fat from the top. Pour into a rigid container, cover, seal and freeze for up to 6 months. Thaw for 3 to 4 hours at room temperature. Reheat gently until very hot. Finish as directed.

∴M·E·N·U∴

· 7 ·

Low-cost Family Meal for 4

Curried Mince
Curd Cheese and Peas
Cauliflower and Lentils
Nut and Vegetable Salad
Mango Chutney

This is an economical and simple menu idea to serve as a family supper or midweek meal. Minced (ground) meat (called *kheema* in India) is used in a large number of recipes. Use lean mince for the best results.

Using Indian Curd Cheese
Indian Curd Cheese and Peas is another favourite dish featuring in most restaurant menus. The cheese used, *panir*, is a curd cheese, and easy to make at home. Do not be tempted to use the soft curd cheese sold in the shops because it dissolves during cooking. It is well worth taking the time to make your own *panir*. It can also be added to soups and vegetable dishes for added protein.

Preparing a coconut
The coconut for the recipe can be bought at supermarkets or Asian food shops. To prepare a coconut, first pierce two of the 'eyes', or little depressions, with a skewer and pour away the liquid. Put the coconut in a preheated oven (190°C/375°F), Gas Mark 5 for 15 minutes. Wrap it in a cloth or duster and place it on a sturdy table or on the floor, and give it a sharp crack with a hammer. It should break in half. Cut out the flesh from the shell, peel away the brown skin and grate the white flesh – either by hand or in a food processor.

Curried Mince

Metric/Imperial	American
2 tablespoons oil	2 tablespoons oil
1 onion, finely chopped	1 onion, finely chopped
1 clove garlic, peeled and crushed	1 clove garlic, peeled and crushed
2 teaspoons ground ginger	2 teaspoons ground ginger
750 g/1½ lb minced beef	3 cups ground beef
1 tablespoon garam masala (page 37)	1 tablespoon garam masala (page 37)
½ teaspoon chilli powder	½ teaspoon chili powder
250 g/8 oz tomatoes, peeled and chopped	1 cup tomatoes, peeled and chopped
2 tablespoons tomato purée	2 tablespoons tomato paste
150 ml/¼ pint beef stock	⅔ cup beef stock
freshly ground black pepper	freshly ground black pepper
300 ml/½ pint natural yogurt	1¼ cups unflavored yogurt

1. Heat the oil in a large saucepan and sauté the onion and garlic until golden. Stir in the ginger, meat, garam masala and chilli powder, and sauté, stirring, until the meat is browned.
2. Stir in the tomatoes, tomato purée (paste), stock, pepper to taste, and half the yogurt. Cover and simmer over low heat for about 40 minutes or until the meat is cooked. Taste and adjust the seasoning, if necessary. Stir in the remaining yogurt. Serve on a bed of plain boiled rice. ·4·

Curd Cheese and Peas

Metric/Imperial	American
125 g/4 oz ghee (page 8) or butter	½ cup ghee (page 8) or butter
500 g/1 lb panir (page 32), cubed	1 lb panir (page 32), cubed
1 onion, sliced	1 onion, sliced
1 teaspoon ground ginger	1 teaspoon ground ginger
½ teaspoon ground cumin	½ teaspoon ground cumin
½ teaspoon chilli powder	½ teaspoon chili powder
½ teaspoon salt	½ teaspoon salt
500 g/1 lb frozen peas	3 cups frozen peas
2 tomatoes, peeled and chopped	2 tomatoes, peeled and chopped

1. Melt the ghee or butter in a frying pan (skillet) and sauté the panir until brown. Remove from the pan with a slotted spoon, drain on absorbent kitchen paper and set aside.
2. Add the onion to the pan and sauté gently until soft. Add the spices and salt and sauté for a further 3 minutes, stirring constantly to keep the spices from burning and sticking.
3. Add the peas and tomatoes; stir gently until the peas are coated with the spice mixture. Stir in the panir with a wooden spoon and heat, taking great care not to break up the cheese cubes. Serve hot. ·12·

Cauliflower and Lentils

Metric/Imperial	American
125 g/4 oz lentils, washed	½ cup lentils, washed
3 tablespoons oil	3 tablespoons oil
2 onions, chopped	2 onions, chopped
2 cloves garlic, peeled and finely chopped	2 cloves garlic, peeled and finely chopped
1 tablespoon grated fresh root ginger	1 tablespoon grated fresh gingerroot
1 teaspoon ground turmeric	1 teaspoon ground turmeric
1 teaspoon ground cumin	1 teaspoon ground cumin
1 tablespoon ground coriander	1 tablespoon ground coriander
½-1 teaspoon chilli powder	½-1 teaspoon chili powder
600 ml/1 pint water	2½ cups water
50 g/2 oz salted peanuts	¼ cup salted peanuts
25 g/1 oz desiccated coconut	⅓ cup shredded coconut
1 medium cauliflower, divided into florets	1 medium cauliflower, divided into flowerets
juice of ½ lemon	juice of ½ lemon
salt	salt

1. Place the lentils in a saucepan, cover with cold water. Bring to the boil; simmer for 5 minutes. Drain.
2. Heat the oil in a saucepan and sauté the onions, garlic and ginger until softened. Stir in the turmeric, cumin, coriander and chilli and cook, stirring, for 5 minutes. Add the water, peanuts, coconut and drained lentils. Bring to the boil, cover and simmer for 15 minutes.
3. Stir in the cauliflower, lemon juice and salt to taste. Cover and simmer for 20 to 25 minutes.

Nut and Vegetable Salad

Metric/Imperial
250 g/8 oz bean sprouts
125 g/4 oz cabbage, shredded
1 green chilli, seeded and very finely chopped
15 g/½ oz fresh root ginger, peeled and finely chopped

American
4 cups beansprouts
1½ cups cabbage, shredded
1 green chili, seeded and very finely chopped
½ oz fresh gingerroot, peeled and finely chopped
2-3 sprigs coriander leaves, chopped

2-3 sprigs coriander leaves, chopped
½ cucumber, grated
lemon juice, to taste
1 apple or 1 ripe mango, peeled and grated
50 g/2 oz unsalted peanuts, roughly chopped
50 g/2 oz unsalted cashew nuts, roughly chopped
½ coconut, flesh removed and grated (page 29)

½ cucumber, grated
lemon juice, to taste
1 apple or 1 ripe mango, peeled and grated
¼ cup unsalted peanuts, roughly chopped
¼ cup unsalted cashew nuts, roughly chopped
½ coconut, flesh removed and grated (page 29)

1. Mix together the bean sprouts, cabbage, chilli, ginger and coriander leaves in a large bowl.
2. Discard any liquid and add the cucumber to the bean-sprout mixture. Sprinkle with salt and lemon juice to taste.
3. Mix the apple or mango with the nuts and coconut. Add to the salad and toss well. ·8·

Mango chutney; Nut and vegetable salad

Mango Chutney

Metric/Imperial	American
6 green mangoes	*6 green mangoes*
about 2 teaspoons salt	*about 2 teaspoons salt*
3-4 red chillis, seeded and roughly chopped, or 2 teaspoons chilli powder	*3-4 red chilis, seeded and roughly chopped, or 2 teaspoons chili powder*
300 ml/½ pint vinegar	*1¼ cups vinegar*
400 g/14 oz sugar	*1¾ cups sugar*
40 g/1½ oz fresh root ginger, peeled and chopped	*1½ oz fresh gingerroot, peeled and chopped*
125 g/4 oz mixed unsalted nuts and raisins, chopped	*¼ lb mixed unsalted nuts and raisins, chopped*

1. Peel the mangoes and grate the flesh into a bowl. Sprinkle with the salt and set aside for 30 minutes.
2. Grind the chillis or mix the chilli powder with a little of the vinegar to a fine paste. Place the remaining vinegar in a saucepan, add the sugar and gently simmer, stirring, until the sugar dissolves.
3. Squeeze the grated mangoes to get rid of any liquid. Add the mango flesh to the pan and gently simmer for a further 5 to 6 minutes. Add the ginger and the chilli paste and mix well. Cook for a further 10 to 12 minutes.
4. Taste and add more salt if necessary. Stir in the chopped nuts and raisins and cook for 4 minutes. Allow to cool. Bottle in airtight jars with vinegar-proof tops. ·2·13·

Homemade Panir:

To make panir, bring 1.2 litres/2 pints (5 cups) milk to the boil. Remove from the heat and leave to cool to blood heat (37°C/98.4°F) or barely warm to the touch. Beat in 150 ml/5 fl oz (⅔ cup) natural (unflavored) yogurt, 2 teaspoons lemon juice and 1½ teaspoons salt. Leave in a warm place for 12 hours or overnight. Line a strainer with muslin (cheesecloth) and place it over a bowl. Pour in the curd mixture and leave to drip for 30 minutes. Gather up the muslin and squeeze out as much of the whey as possible. Shape the cheese into a round and drape the muslin ends over the top; put on the draining board of the sink with a weight – a saucepan filled with water is best – on top. Leave for 3 hours. Cut the cheese into cubes and use as directed.

C · O · U · N · T · D · O · W · N

The week before:
Make the mango chutney and store in a cool place.
Two days before:
Boil the milk for the panir. Cool, stir in the other ingredients, cover and leave in a warm place.
The day before:
Finish making the panir and press it. Cut into cubes and keep covered in the refrigerator. Make the curried mince. Cool, cover and refrigerate. Break open the coconut and grate the flesh. Refrigerate.
On the day:
Prepare the cauliflower and onions and the salad vegetables. Cover and refrigerate.
To serve at 8 pm:
6.00: Make the cauliflower and lentils.
7.00: Prepare the indian curd cheese and peas.
7.30: Make the nut and vegetable salad. Spoon the mango chutney into a serving bowl.
7.40: Skim off any fat from the top of the curried mince. Reheat and serve.
8.00: Take the dishes to the table.

F · R · E · E · Z · E · R · N · O · T · E · S

Make the Curried Mince. Cool quickly and skim off any fat from the top. Spoon into a rigid container, cover, seal and freeze for up to 2 months. To serve, thaw at room temperature for 3 to 4 hours. Heat gently until very hot. Prepare the Cauliflower and Lentils, but slightly undercook. Cool quickly and spoon into a rigid container. Cover, seal and freeze for up to 3 months. To serve, thaw at room temperature for 3 to 4 hours. Heat gently until hot.

⸚M·E·N·U⸚

· 8 ·

Formal Dinner for 6 to 8

Spiced Roast Leg of Lamb
Kashmiri Pilau
Savoury Fruit Salad
Tomato and Yogurt Relish
Curd and Saffron Pudding

This is an impressive dinner menu, simple to prepare and serve. The main dish is a delicious whole leg of lamb, covered in a spice paste and roasted in the oven, called *raan* in India. In the days before modern cooking ranges, *raan* was cooked over a charcoal or wood fire with hot coals placed on the lid of the pan. The spiced lamb emerges from the oven so tender and succulent that it just lifts off the bone.

Using Chillis

Fresh chillis, usually green or red, come in many shapes and sizes. Only the red are dried and available whole, coarsely ground or powdered. As a rule, the smaller and thinner the chilli the hotter it is. The tiny 'bird's-eye' chilli, usually only available in South-East Asian shops, is the most pungent. The larger, thin green chillis are not quite as hot. The pungency, however, is variable and it is wise to be cautious. To prepare fresh chillis, wash them in cold water, cut off the stalks and, if the seeds (they are the hotter part) are to be removed, slit the chillis in half lengthways. Remove the seeds with the tip of the knife, then chop the chillis. For dried chillis, either use them whole or crumble them between your fingertips or between 2 teaspoons. Chillis can burn the skin and eyes, so DO NOT touch your face or rub your eyes while handling them, and wash your hands immediately afterwards.

Spiced Roast Leg of Lamb

Metric/Imperial
150 g/5 oz fresh ginger
8-10 cloves garlic, peeled
2 green chillis, chopped
2 teaspoons cumin seeds
20 cloves
1 teaspoon peppercorns
3 large cardamoms
8 small green cardamoms
3-4 sprigs coriander leaves
3 tablespoons lemon juice
1 tablespoon vinegar
150 ml/1/4 pint natural
    yogurt
1/2 teaspoon chilli powder
2 teaspoons ground

American
5 oz fresh gingerroot
8-10 cloves garlic, peeled
2 green chilis, chopped
2 teaspoons cumin seeds
20 cloves
1 teaspoon peppercorns
3 large cardamoms
8 small green cardamoms
3-4 sprigs coriander leaves
3 tablespoons lemon juice
1 tablespoon vinegar
2/3 cup unflavored yogurt
1/2 teaspoon chili powder
2 teaspoons ground
    coriander

coriander
2 teaspoons paprika
1.75 kg/4-41/4 lb leg of
    lamb, trimmed
salt
To Garnish:
lime slices
fresh mint sprigs
fried onion rings

2 teaspoons paprika
4-41/4 lb leg of lamb,
    trimmed
salt
To Garnish:
lime slices
fresh mint sprigs
fried onion rings

1. Put the ginger, garlic, green chillis, cumin seeds, cloves, peppercorns, large and small cardamoms and coriander leaves with the lemon juice in a blender or food processor and work to a smooth paste. Mix in the vinegar and yogurt, then add the chilli powder, coriander and paprika.
2. Make 2.5 cm/1 inch deep cuts across the meat and sprinkle with salt. Put the lamb in a bowl. Pour over the spice and yogurt mixture and rub it into the cuts. Cover with cling film (plastic wrap) and leave

Spiced roast leg of lamb

to marinate in the refrigerator for 48 hours.

3. Take the lamb out of the refrigerator and place in a large flameproof casserole with the marinade. Bring to the boil on top of the cooker. Transfer to a preheated oven (220°C/425°F), Gas Mark 7 and bake uncovered for 30 minutes. Reduce the oven temperature to 160°C/325°F, Gas Mark 3. Cover and cook for 3½ hours, basting occasionally.

4. Remove the meat from the casserole and keep on a serving dish covered with foil. Put the casserole on top of the cooker, skim off any fat from the top, and simmer the sauce until thick. Pour over the lamb. Carve, garnish and serve. ·13·

Kashmiri Pilau

Metric/Imperial	American
500 g/1 lb basmati or long-grain rice	2²/₃ cups basmati or long-grain rice
75 g/3 oz ghee (page 8) or butter	¹/₃ cup ghee (page 8) or butter
5 whole cardamoms	5 whole cardamoms
5 bay leaves	5 bay leaves
¹/₂ stick cinnamon	¹/₂ stick cinnamon
8 whole cloves	8 whole cloves
1 teaspoon cumin seeds	1 teaspoon cumin seeds
1.2 litre/2 pints water	5 cups water
walnut halves, to garnish	walnut halves, to garnish

1. Wash the rice and soak in cold water for 30 minutes, then drain thoroughly.

2. Heat the ghee or butter in a large saucepan and sauté the cardamoms, bay leaves, cinnamon, cloves and cumin seeds until slightly brown. Add the rice and cook until the grains are transparent, stirring them.

3. Add the water, bring to the boil, cover and simmer until the liquid is absorbed, about 25 minutes.

4. Dry the rice, uncovered, in the oven. Garnish with walnut halves before serving.

Savoury Fruit Salad

Metric/Imperial	American
2 oranges	2 oranges
2 bananas	2 bananas
2 pears	2 pears
1 apple	1 apple
2 guavas (optional)	2 guavas (optional)
juice of 1 lemon	juice of 1 lemon
2 teaspoons chilli powder	2 teaspoons chili powder
1 teaspoon ground ginger	1 teaspoon ground ginger
1 teaspoon garam masala (page 37)	1 teaspoon garam masala (page 37)
1 teaspoon salt	1 teaspoon salt
¹/₂ teaspoon freshly ground black pepper	¹/₂ teaspoon freshly ground black pepper

1. Peel the oranges and bananas and chop roughly. Core the pears and apple, and chop roughly with the guavas, if using. (Do not discard the guava seeds.)

2. Put the fruit in a bowl and sprinkle with the lemon juice. Mix together the chilli powder, ginger, garam masala and salt and pepper to taste. Sprinkle over the fruit, then toss lightly to coat each piece.

3. Chill the salad for 2 hours before serving.

Tomato and Yogurt Relish

Metric/Imperial	American
2-4 green chillis, seeded and very finely chopped	2-4 green chilis, seeded and very finely chopped
1 teaspoon salt	1 teaspoon salt
¹/₂ teaspoon sugar	¹/₂ teaspoon sugar
50 g/2 oz desiccated coconut	¹/₂ cup shredded coconut
300 ml/¹/₂ pint natural yogurt	1¹/₄ cups unflavored yogurt
500 g/1 lb tomatoes, peeled and chopped	1 lb tomatoes, peeled and chopped
juice of ¹/₂ lemon	juice of ¹/₂ lemon
1 tablespoon oil	1 tablespoon oil
2 teaspoons mustard seeds	2 teaspoons mustard seeds

1. Mix together the chillis, salt, sugar, coconut and half the yogurt in a bowl. Set aside for 1 hour.
2. Stir in the tomatoes, lemon juice and enough of the remaining yogurt to give a thick consistency. (The coconut should swell and thicken the mixture.)
3. Heat the oil in a small frying pan (skillet) and sauté the mustard seeds. As soon as they begin to splutter, tip the seeds and oil into the relish. Mix well, cover and chill in the refrigerator. ·7·

Curd and Saffron Pudding

Metric/Imperial	American
500 g/1 lb full-fat curd cheese	2 cups cottage cheese
125 g/4 oz full-fat soft cheese	1/2 cup cream cheese
150 ml/1/4 pint natural yogurt	2/3 cup unflavored yogurt
125-175 g/4-6 oz icing sugar, sifted	1-1 1/2 cups confectioners' sugar, sifted
10-15 small green cardamoms, shelled and seeds ground	10-15 small green cardamoms, shelled and seeds ground
pinch of ground saffron	pinch of ground saffron
To Decorate:	To Decorate:
25 g/1 oz slivered almonds	2 tablespoons slivered almonds
15 g/1/2 oz pistachio nuts, sliced	1 tablespoon pistachio nuts, sliced

1. Beat the cheeses and yogurt in a bowl until smooth. Gradually add the sugar and continue beating until light and fluffy. Stir in the ground cardamoms and saffron with a metal spoon.
2. Pour into individual serving dishes and decorate with the sliced nuts. Chill well in the refrigerator before serving. ·9·

Cooking Rice:
A good way to boil rice is the evaporation method which retains all the goodness in the rice. First measure the rice in a cup or measuring jug. For every cup of rice you will need 1 1/2 cups of water at the very most. Wash the rice and leave to soak for 30 minutes. Drain the rice and put in a saucepan with the measured water and a little salt. Bring the rice to the boil, cover tightly and turn down the heat to very low. Cook for 20 to 25 minutes or until all the liquid has been absorbed and the rice is tender and light. (Do not uncover during cooking time).

C · O · U · N · T · D · O · W · N
Two days before:
Prepare the marinade and rub it all over the leg of lamb. Place the lamb in a bowl, cover with cling film (plastic wrap) and store in the refrigerator.
The day before:
Make the tomato and yogurt relish. Cover and refrigerate. Make the curd and saffron pudding. Cover and refrigerate.
On the day:
Cook the kashmiri pilau. Transfer to a lightly greased ovenproof serving dish, cover tightly with lightly greased foil and a lid.
To serve at 8 pm:
3.20: Preheat the oven to 220°C/425°F, Gas Mark 7.
3.40: Put the lamb to roast.
5.00: Make the savoury fruit salad. Cover and refrigerate.
7.30: Reheat the kashmiri pilau in the oven. Place the relish in a serving bowl.
7.40: Take the lamb out of the oven, cover and leave to rest. Thicken the sauce and pour over the lamb before serving.
8.00: Carve and garnish the lamb. Garnish the pilau. Take the savoury dishes to the table.

F · R · E · E · Z · E · R · N · O · T · E · S
The spice paste marinade for the leg of lamb can be frozen for up to 6 months. When required, thaw at room temperature for 5 to 6 hours or until quite soft and pliable.

∴M∆E∆N∆U∴

· 9 ·

Light Lunch for 4

Fried Spiced Fish
Beef in Yogurt Sauce
Spiced Sweetcorn
Curried Potatoes
Chick Pea Fudge

Serve the tempting fried fish as a first course, accompanied by a cucumber salad – dressed with seasoned wine vinegar, garnished with chopped green chilli – and wholemeal toast or French bread. Alternatively, serve the fish instead of the beef in yogurt sauce for a vegetarian meal.

The main course of beef, sweetcorn and potatoes may be served with *naan* (page 63), apricot or mango chutney (page 28 or 32).

A Sweetmeat to Finish

Serve the nutty chick pea fudge as a sweet snack to finish the meal, or offer a fruit salad or a tangy lemon or orange sorbet (sherbet).

Garam Masala

Beef in yogurt sauce includes a spice blend called *garam masala*. This is used in many recipes and is available in supermarkets and all Asian grocers' shops. It is also easy to make – homemade garam masala is superior in flavour and aroma and will keep for 6 months.

Although no 2 recipes for garam masala are the same, here is an easy one to try: put 1 tablespoon cumin seeds, 1 tablespoon cardamom pods, 1 tablespoon black peppercorns, 1 tablespoon coriander seeds, 2 teaspoons whole cloves and 2 medium cinnamon sticks into a coffee grinder, or use a pestle and mortar or a rolling pin, and grind to a powder.

Fried Spiced Fish

Metric/Imperial	American
about 1 teaspoon chilli powder	*about 1 teaspoon chili powder*
1 teaspoon ground cumin	*1 teaspoon ground cumin*
lemon juice	*lemon juice*
salt	*salt*
freshly ground black pepper	*freshly ground black pepper*
4 × 175 g/6 oz white fish fillets, e.g. haddock or cod, rinsed and dried	*4 × 6 oz white fish fillets, e.g. haddock or cod, rinsed and dried*
50 g/2 oz coriander leaves	*2 oz coriander leaves*
1 clove garlic, peeled	*1 clove garlic, peeled*
1 green chilli, seeded	*1 green chili, seeded*
1 teaspoon garam masala (page 37)	*1 teaspoon garam masala (page 37)*
oil, for frying	*oil, for frying*
lime or lemon wedges, to garnish	*lime or lemon wedges, to garnish*

1. Mix together the chilli powder, cumin, 2 teaspoons lemon juice and salt and pepper to taste. Sprinkle over the fish fillets.
2. Purée the coriander leaves, garlic and chilli in a blender. If too thick, add a spoonful of lemon juice. Rub this mixture well into the fish and sprinkle with the garam masala. Set aside for 10 minutes.
3. Heat a little oil and sauté the fish, two at a time, for about 5 minutes on each side. Keep warm while cooking the rest. Serve hot, garnished with lime or lemon wedges.

Beef in Yogurt Sauce

Metric/Imperial	American
500 g/1 lb beef, thinly sliced	*1 lb beef, thinly sliced*
1 teaspoon salt	*1 teaspoon salt*
300 ml/¹⁄₂ pint natural yogurt	*1¹⁄₄ cups unflavored yogurt*
	³⁄₄ cup ghee (page 8) or butter
175 g/6 oz ghee (page 8) or butter	*1 large onion, sliced*
1 large onion, sliced	*3 cloves garlic, peeled and sliced*
3 cloves garlic, peeled and sliced	*1¹⁄₂ teaspoons ground ginger*
1¹⁄₂ teaspoons ground ginger	*2 teaspoons ground coriander*
2 teaspoons ground coriander	*2 teaspoons chili powder*
2 teaspoons chilli powder	*¹⁄₂ teaspoon ground cumin*
¹⁄₂ teaspoon ground cumin	*1 teaspoon ground turmeric*
1 teaspoon ground turmeric	*1 teaspoon garam masala (page 37)*
1 teaspoon garam masala (page 37)	

1. Put the beef between two sheets greaseproof (waxed) paper and tenderize with a mallet. Rub the beef with the salt, then put in a bowl and cover with the yogurt. Leave to marinate overnight.
2. Melt the ghee or butter in a heavy saucepan and sauté the onion and garlic for 3 minutes, stirring.
3. Add the beef and marinade to the pan together with the ginger, coriander, chilli powder, cumin and turmeric, stir well. Cover the pan with a tight-fitting lid and simmer for 1¹⁄₂ hours or until the meat is tender. Sprinkle with the garam masala. ·5·

Spiced Sweetcorn

Metric/Imperial	American
40 g/1¹⁄₂ oz ghee (page 8) or 3 tablespoons oil	*3 tablespoons ghee (page 8) or oil*
1 small onion, chopped	*1 small onion, chopped*
1 medium potato, peeled and cubed	*1 medium potato, peeled and cubed*
2 green chillis, halved and seeded	*2 green chilis, halved and seeded*
5-6 curry leaves	*5-6 curry leaves*
175 g/6 oz sweetcorn kernels	*1¹⁄₂ cups whole kernel corn*
¹⁄₂ teaspoon chilli powder	*¹⁄₂ teaspoon chili powder*
	1 teaspoon ground coriander

1 teaspoon ground coriander
1/2 teaspoon ground turmeric
salt
1 × 225 g/8 oz can
  tomatoes
2-3 sprigs coriander leaves,
  chopped
1 teaspoon garam masala
  (page 37)
lemon juice

1/2 teaspoon ground turmeric
salt
1 × 8 oz can tomatoes
2-3 sprigs coriander leaves,
  chopped
1 teaspoon garam masala
  (page 37)
lemon juice

1. Heat the ghee or oil in a saucepan and sauté the onion until just tender. Add the potato and continue cooking for 4 to 5 minutes, then stir in the chillis, curry leaves, sweetcorn, chilli powder, coriander and turmeric, and sauté for 3 to 5 minutes until the mixture is dry.
2. Add salt to taste and the tomatoes, cover and cook for 5 to 8 minutes until the potatoes are tender and the sauce has thickened. Stir in the chopped coriander leaves, garam masala and lemon juice to taste.

Curried Potatoes

Metric/Imperial
500 g/1 lb small new
  potatoes
1 medium onion, quartered
25 g/1 oz fresh root ginger,
  peeled and cut in pieces
4 tablespoons oil
about 1 teaspoon chilli
  powder
1/2 teaspoon ground
  turmeric
1/2 teaspoon sugar
salt
150 ml/1/4 pint water
1 1/2 teaspoons garam
  masala (page 37)
chopped coriander leaves, to
  garnish

American
1 lb small new potatoes
1 medium onion, quartered
1 oz fresh gingerroot, peeled
  and cut in pieces
4 tablespoons oil
about 1 teaspoon chili
  powder
1/2 teaspoon ground turmeric
1/2 teaspoon sugar
salt
2/3 cup water
1 1/2 teaspoons garam
  masala (page 37)
chopped coriander leaves, to
  garnish

Chick pea fudge

1. Put the potatoes in a saucepan, cover with water and boil until just tender. Drain.
2. Purée the onion and ginger in a blender. Heat the oil in a pan and sauté the onion and ginger purée until light brown. Stir in the chilli powder, turmeric, sugar and salt. Cook for 1 to 2 minutes, without letting the mixture burn; add the water.
3. When the water begins to simmer, stir in the potatoes, cover and cook until the sauce has thickened. Sprinkle with the garam masala. Garnish with coriander leaves before serving. ·4·

Chick Pea Fudge

Metric/Imperial	American
350 g/12 oz unsalted butter or ghee (page 8)	1½ cups unsalted butter or ghee (page 8)
300 g/10 oz chick pea flour (besan), sifted	2 cups chick pea flour (besan), sifted
300 ml/½ pint water	1¼ cups water
350 g/12 oz sugar	1½ cups sugar
pinch of salt	pinch of salt
10 small green cardamoms, shelled and seeds ground	10 small green cardamoms, shelled and seeds ground
30 g/1¼ oz mixed unsalted nuts, sliced, e.g. almonds, pistachio and cashew	2 tablespoons mixed unsalted sliced nuts, e.g. almonds, pistachio and cashew

1. Grease a 20 × 25 cm/8 × 10 inch baking dish. Using a nonstick or heavy-based saucepan, melt the butter or ghee and gently fry the chick pea flour for 5 to 6 minutes, stirring constantly, until light brown. Remove from the heat and set aside.
2. To make a thick sugar syrup, place the water and sugar in a saucepan. Heat until the sugar dissolves, then boil for 5 minutes or until the syrup is light golden and has thickened. If a small spoonful is taken out and cooled slightly it should form a single strand between the finger and thumb. If the syrup becomes too thick, add a little water.

3. Add the fried flour to the syrup and cook over low heat for 10 to 15 minutes, stirring constantly, until the mixture comes away from the sides of the pan and forms a ball.
4. Remove from the heat; stir in the salt, cardamom and nuts. Pour into the greased dish and smooth the surface with a wet spatula. Leave to cool before cutting and serving. Cut into cubes or diamond shapes for serving. ·8·

C · O · U · N · T · D · O · W · N

Two days before:
Prepare the beef, put it in a bowl with the yogurt, cover with cling film (plastic wrap) and refrigerate overnight.

The day before:
Cook the beef. Cool, cover with cling film (plastic wrap) and refrigerate. Make the chick pea fudge and store in an airtight container.

On the day:
Prepare the vegetables for the spiced sweetcorn and curried potatoes. Cover the potatoes with cold water.

To serve at 1 pm:
11.00: Cook the spiced sweetcorn.
11.30: Prepare the curried potatoes. Skim off any fat from the top of the beef.
12 noon: Coat the fish and marinate.
12.30: Reheat the beef on top of the cooker. Cook the fish.
1.00: Garnish the fish and serve.

F · R · E · E · Z · E · R · N · O · T · E · S

Rub the fish all over with the spice paste. Open freeze. When frozen, pack into a rigid container with foil separating each layer. Freeze for up to 3 months. To serve, cook from frozen for 6 minutes on each side or until cooked through. Cook the beef. Cool quickly, skim off any fat from the top. Spoon into a rigid container, cover, seal and freeze for up to 2 months. To serve, thaw overnight in the refrigerator and heat gently.

⠆M⋅E⋅N⋅U⠆

· 10 ·

Tandoori Meal for 4

Prawn and Egg Sambal
Tandoori Chicken
Potatoes with Cumin and Fenugreek
Spicy Fried Okra
Creamed Rice

For relaxed entertaining, Indian food is hard to beat. Most of the main dishes improve on keeping. They can be prepared in advance and reheated before serving. Many can be frozen, too. It is usual when entertaining to include one meat or poultry, one fish, two vegetable and one lentil dish. Accompaniments include rice and/or bread (*chapatis*, *naans*, etc.), poppadoms, relishes and salads, chutneys and pickles, and yogurt, in one form or another. In this country, however, it is quite acceptable to serve just one main dish, for example, the Tandoori chicken in this menu, or chicken curry (page 18) or spiced roast leg of lamb (page 34) accompanied by all the mentioned rice, breads and side dishes.

Traditional Clay Oven

Tandoori Chicken is one of the most popular Indian dishes and a speciality of the Punjab and north west of the country. Its name derives from the oven it is traditionally cooked in. A tandoor is a large clay oven which is heated to high temperatures by charcoal. Meat, poultry, fish and other foods are marinated before being lowered into the oven to bake. This type of oven ensures that foods are crisp and dry on the outside, but tender and succulent inside. *Naan* (page 63), an Indian bread, is pressed on to the walls of the oven to bake. An ordinary oven, barbecue or rotisserie can successfully be used for tandoori dishes.

Prawn and Egg Sambal

Metric/Imperial
500 g/1 lb peeled prawns
4 hard-boiled eggs,
    quartered
300 ml/½ pint coconut
    milk
1 small onion, finely
    chopped
1 clove garlic, peeled and
    crushed
1 green chilli, seeded and
    chopped
juice of ½ lemon
pinch of chilli powder
½ teaspoon salt
To Garnish:
50 g/2 oz cooked green peas
chopped coriander leaves

American
1 lb shelled shrimp
4 hard-cooked eggs,
    quartered
1¼ cups coconut milk
1 small onion, finely
    chopped
1 clove garlic, peeled and
    crushed
1 green chili, seeded and
    chopped
juice of ½ lemon
pinch of chili powder
½ teaspoon salt
To Garnish:
⅓ cup cooked green peas
chopped coriander leaves

1. Arrange the prawns (shrimp) and eggs in a serving dish, then chill in the refrigerator.
2. Work the coconut milk, onion, garlic, green chilli, lemon juice, chilli powder and salt in a blender or food processor until evenly blended.
3. Pour the mixture over the prawns and eggs. Garnish with the peas and coriander. Serve well chilled. ·14·

How to Make Coconut Milk:
Remove the flesh from a coconut (page 29) and grate it by hand or in a food processor. Put the coconut in a bowl and pour in 600 ml/1 pint (2½ cups) boiling water. Leave to infuse for 1 hour, then strain through muslin (cheesecloth). Press and squeeze to extract as much 'milk' as possible. This is called 'thick' coconut milk. Put the coconut residue back into the bowl, pour in another 600 ml/1 pint (2½ cups) boiling water and repeat the process. This is called 'thin' coconut milk.

Tandoori Chicken

Metric/Imperial	American
4 chicken breasts, skinned and boned	4 chicken breasts, skinned and boned
1 teaspoon cayenne	1 teaspoon cayenne
1 teaspoon salt	1 teaspoon salt
juice of $1/2$ lemon	juice of $1/2$ lemon
$1/2$ teaspoon red food colouring (optional)	$1/2$ teaspoon red food coloring (optional)
4 tablespoons natural yogurt	4 tablespoons unflavored yogurt
2 large cloves garlic, peeled	2 large cloves garlic, peeled
1 × 5 cm/2 inch piece fresh root ginger, peeled and cut in pieces	1 × 2 inch piece fresh gingerroot, peeled and cut in pieces
2 teaspoons ground coriander	2 teaspoons ground coriander
lemon or lime quarters, to garnish	lemon or lime quarters, to garnish

1. Using a sharp kitchen knife, make two slits in each chicken breast. Mix together the cayenne, salt, lemon juice, and colouring if using, and rub into the chicken. Set aside.
2. Put 1 tablespoon of the yogurt, the garlic, ginger and coriander into a blender or food processor and blend to a smooth paste. Mix in the remaining yogurt. Pour the yogurt mixture over the chicken breasts and rub it into the slits. Cover with cling film (plastic wrap) and leave to marinate in the refrigerator for 24 hours.
3. Take the chicken out of the refrigerator 2 to 3 hours before cooking. Remove any excess marinade and put the chicken breasts on a rack placed in a shallow baking tray.
4. Bake the chicken in a preheated oven (240°C/475°F), Gas Mark 9 for 20 to 25 minutes or until tender. Garnish with lemon or lime quarters.

Prawn and egg sambal

Potatoes with Cumin and Fenugreek

Metric/Imperial	American
1 teaspoon cumin seeds	1 teaspoon cumin seeds
$1/2$ teaspoon fenugreek seeds	$1/2$ teaspoon fenugreek seeds
2 dried red chillis or 1 teaspoon chilli powder	2 dried red chilis or 1 teaspoon chili powder
1 onion, chopped	1 onion, chopped
25 g/1 oz ghee (page 8) or 2 tablespoons oil	2 tablespoons ghee (page 8) or oil
8-10 curry leaves	8-10 curry leaves
1 teaspoon mustard seeds	1 teaspoon mustard seeds
500 g/1 lb potatoes, boiled, peeled and cut into chunks	1 lb potatoes, boiled, peeled and cut into chunks
salt	salt
$1/2$ teaspoon ground turmeric	$1/2$ teaspoon ground turmeric
1 tablespoon fresh or desiccated coconut	1 tablespoon fresh or shredded coconut

1. Dry-roast the cumin, fenugreek and whole chillis or powder in a non-stick frying pan (skillet) for 1 minute. Add the onion and 2 teaspoons of the oil or ghee and continue frying for 1 minute. Tip the mixture with a little water into a blender or food processor and work to a fine paste.
2. Heat the remaining ghee or oil in a saucepan and sauté the curry leaves and mustard seeds for 30 seconds, then add the spice paste, the potatoes, salt, turmeric and coconut. Add a little water, cover and cook gently for 3 to 4 minutes. ·11·

Optional Extra
Crush 500 g/1 lb hulled strawberries with a fork. Whip two cartons of Greek strained yogurt with 2 tablespoons sugar or clear honey. Fold in the strawberries. Spoon into individual glass bowls, scatter with toasted split almonds and decorate with unhulled whole strawberries.

Spicy Fried Okra

Metric/Imperial	American
125 g/4 oz ghee (page 8) or butter	1/2 cup ghee (page 8) or butter
1 large onion, sliced	1 large onion, sliced
2 cloves garlic, peeled and sliced	2 cloves garlic, peeled and sliced
1 tablespoon ground coriander	1 tablespoon ground coriander
1 teaspoon ground turmeric	1 teaspoon ground turmeric
freshly ground black pepper	freshly ground black pepper
500 g/1 lb fresh okra, topped, tailed and cut into 1 cm/1/2 inch pieces	1 lb fresh okra, trimmed and cut into 1/2 inch pieces
150 ml/1/4 pint water	2/3 cup water
1/2 teaspoon garam masala (page 37)	1/2 teaspoon garam masala (page 37)

1. Melt the ghee or butter in a heavy saucepan and gently sauté the onion and garlic until soft. Add the garlic, coriander, turmeric, and pepper, and sauté, stirring constantly, for a further 3 minutes.
2. Add the okra, then stir gently to coat with the spice mixture, taking care not to break them.
3. Stir in the water and bring to the boil. Lower the heat, cover and simmer for 5 to 10 minutes until the okra are just tender, but still firm to the bite. Stir in the garam masala and serve.

Creamed Rice

Metric/Imperial	American
600 ml/1 pint milk	2 1/2 cups milk
125 g/4 oz sugar	1/2 cup sugar
50 g/2 oz rice flour	1/2 cup rice flour
2 teaspoons chopped pistachio nuts	2 teaspoons chopped pistachio nuts
2 teaspoons blanched slivered almonds	2 teaspoons blanched slivered almonds
1/2 teaspoon rose water	1/2 teaspoon rose water

1. Put the milk in a heavy-based saucepan and bring slowly to the boil. Stir in the sugar, then gradually sprinkle in the rice flour, stirring constantly to prevent lumps from forming.
2. Add the nuts and cook until the mixture begins to thicken, stirring constantly.
3. Remove from the heat, stir in the rose water and cool. Serve cold. ·14·

C · O · U · N · T · D · O · W · N

The day before:
Prepare the spice paste for the Tandoori chicken. Spread it over the chicken breasts, cover and refrigerate overnight. Make the creamed rice and keep covered in the refrigerator.

On the day:
Make the prawn and egg sambal. Cover and keep in the refrigerator. Boil the potatoes, cool, cover and refrigerate. Prepare the vegetables for the spicy fried okra.

To serve at 8 pm:
About 5.00: Remove the Tandoori chicken from the refrigerator. Set aside and allow to come to room temperature.
6.30: Prepare the potatoes with cumin and fenugreek.
7.10: Preheat the oven. Prepare the spicy fried okra.
7.30: Bake the Tandoori chicken in the oven. Take the creamed rice out of the refrigerator.
8.00: Garnish the dishes. Serve the prawn and egg sambal.

F · R · E · E · Z · E · R · N · O · T · E · S

Cover the chicken breasts with the spice paste. Open freeze. Wrap each breast in foil, pack into a rigid container, seal and freeze for up to 2 months. To serve, thaw in the refrigerator overnight. Then cook as directed. If preferred, freeze only the spice paste. It will keep in the freezer for up to 6 months. Thaw the spice paste in the refrigerator overnight before using.

⁖M⁘E⁘N⁘U⁖

· 11 ·

Outdoor Eating for 4

Tikka Kebabs
Prawn Curry
Spiced Spinach
Tomatoes with Ginger
Green Beans with Coconut

A North Indian Speciality

Tikka kebabs (kabobs) are traditionally cooked over charcoal on street corners in north Indian towns during the cold winter months, but are the ideal barbecue dish for entertaining on long summer evenings. Although best when cooked over charcoal, the kebabs are very satisfactorily cooked under a grill (broiler).

The prawn curry and remaining dishes are quick and easy to prepare and can be made in advance as they don't spoil by being kept waiting and reheating. Serve all the dishes together in the Indian style with additional accompaniments such as mango or banana chutney (page 32 or 12), and raita with tiny pakoras (page 20) set out on a small table for guests to help themselves. Or, if you prefer, serve the kebabs as a first course with *naan* (page 63), then the other dishes together with plain boiled rice (page 36).

The Best Drinks

A common dilemma when serving spicy food is what to offer your guests to drink. Even the most robust wines are lost among the strength of Indian flavours. Well chilled lager, or a refreshing soft drink like homemade lemonade is best; plus large jugs of ice-cold mineral water with slices of lemon or lime.

Tikka Kebabs

Metric/Imperial

500 g/1 lb boned lamb shoulder or leg, cut into 2.5 cm/1 inch cubes
juice of 1 lemon
150 ml/¼ pint natural yogurt
4 small onions, quartered
3 cloves garlic, chopped
½ teaspoon ground turmeric
1 tablespoon vinegar
½ teaspoon salt
1 teaspoon freshly ground black pepper
1 green pepper, seeded and cut into 2.5 cm/1 inch squares
lemon quarters, to garnish

American

1 lb boneless lamb shoulder or leg, cut into 1 inch cubes
juice of 1 lemon
⅔ cup unflavored yogurt
4 small onions, quartered
3 cloves garlic, chopped
½ teaspoon ground turmeric
1 tablespoon vinegar
½ teaspoon salt
1 teaspoon freshly ground black pepper
1 green pepper, seeded and cut into 1 inch squares
lemon quarters, to garnish

1. Put the lamb in a bowl and sprinkle with the lemon juice. Put the yogurt, half the onion, the garlic, turmeric, vinegar and salt and pepper in a blender or food processor and work until the mixture is evenly blended. Pour over the lamb and stir well. Cover and leave to marinate in the refrigerator overnight.

2. Separate the remaining onion quarters into layers. Thread the cubes of meat on to eight kebab (kabob) skewers, alternating with the green pepper pieces and onion.

3. Barbecue or grill (broil) the kebabs for about 10 minutes, turning frequently, until tender. Serve hot, garnished with lemon quarters. ·3·

Variation:

For a colourful effect, use red and yellow peppers as well as the green pepper. The extra pieces can be used as a garnish.

Tikka kebabs

Prawn Curry

Metric/Imperial	American
2 tablespoons oil	2 tablespoons oil
1 onion, diced	1 onion, diced
500 g/1 lb peeled prawns	1 lb shelled shrimp
3 cloves garlic, peeled and crushed	3 cloves garlic, peeled and crushed
1½ teaspoons garam masala (page 37)	1½ teaspoons garam masala (page 37)
about 1½ teaspoons chilli powder	about 1½ teaspoons chili powder
½ teaspoon ground turmeric	½ teaspoon ground turmeric
salt	salt
200 ml/⅓ pint water	1 cup water
To Garnish:	To Garnish:
1-2 green chillis, seeded and very finely chopped	1-2 green chilis, seeded and very finely chopped
2-3 sprigs coriander leaves, chopped	2-3 sprigs coriander leaves, chopped
lemon juice	lemon juice
1-2 tomatoes, sliced	1-2 tomatoes, sliced

1. Heat the oil in a saucepan and gently sauté the onion until tender. Add the prawns (shrimp) and continue cooking until the mixture is completely dry. Keep stirring to prevent the prawns and onions from sticking to the saucepan.
2. Add the garlic, garam masala, chilli powder and turmeric, stir well and sauté for 30 seconds. Add salt to taste and the water. Cover and cook gently for 10 to 15 minutes until dry.
3. Garnish with the chopped chilli and coriander leaves, then sprinkle with lemon juice to taste and arrange the tomato slices on top. Serve with *naan* (page 63). ·14·

Cook's Tip:
If you are using uncooked prawns add them after the onion is sautéed and cook until they become pink and opaque, then add the other ingredients.

Spiced Spinach

Metric/Imperial	American
50 g/2 oz ghee (page 8) or butter	¼ cup ghee (page 8) or butter
1 small onion, sliced	1 small onion, sliced
1 teaspoon garam masala (page 37)	1 teaspoon garam masala (page 37)
1 teaspoon salt	1 teaspoon salt
500 g/1 lb frozen whole-leaf spinach	1 lb frozen whole-leaf spinach

1. Melt the ghee or butter in a heavy saucepan and gently sauté the onion until soft. Add the garam masala and salt and sauté, stirring constantly, for a further 3 minutes.
2. Add the frozen spinach and cook for about 5 minutes, stirring constantly, until thawed and heated through. Serve hot. ·10·

Tomatoes with Ginger

Metric/Imperial	American
2 onions, quartered	2 onions, quartered
2 cloves garlic, peeled	2 cloves garlic, peeled
1 × 3.5 cm/1½ inch piece fresh root ginger, peeled	1 × 1½ inch piece fresh gingerroot, peeled
2 green chillis, seeded	2 green chilis, seeded
3 tablespoons oil	3 tablespoons oil
750 g/1½ lb tomatoes, peeled and chopped	1½ lb tomatoes, peeled and chopped
1 tablespoon desiccated coconut	1 tablespoon shredded coconut
salt	salt

1. Put the onions, garlic, ginger and chillis in a blender or food processor and work to a smooth paste.
2. Heat the oil in a saucepan and sauté the spice paste, stirring, for 10 to 15 minutes. If the mixture gets too dry, add 1 to 2 tablespoons water.

3. Add the tomatoes, coconut and salt to taste. Cover and simmer for 15 minutes. If the mixture is too thin, simmer uncovered for a few minutes until the sauce thickens. ·6·

Green Beans with Coconut

Metric/Imperial	American
50 g/2 oz ghee (page 8) or 4 tablespoons oil	4 tablespoons ghee (page 8) or oil
2 red or green chillis	2 red or green chilis
6-7 curry leaves	6-7 curry leaves
250 g/8 oz potatoes, peeled and diced	1/2 lb potatoes, peeled and diced
500 g/1 lb green beans, sliced	1 lb green beans, sliced
salt	salt
1 tablespoon desiccated coconut	1 tablespoon shredded coconut
To Garnish:	To Garnish:
fresh coriander leaves	fresh coriander leaves
25 g/1 oz slivered almonds	1/4 cup slivered almonds

1. Heat the ghee or oil in a saucepan and sauté the whole chillis and curry leaves for a few minutes. Add the potatoes and continue cooking for 6 minutes.
2. Add the green beans and coconut. Cover and cook for 3 to 4 minutes. Stir and cook for a further 5 minutes or until the potatoes are tender. Garnish the green beans with the coriander leaves and almonds before serving. ·5·

Optional Extra:
Make a refreshing sorbet (sherbet) from lychees. You will need 2 × 500 g/1 lb cans of lychees. Drain them and put the syrup in a small saucepan. Stir in 2 tablespoons caster sugar and, when it has dissolved, boil rapidly until the syrup is reduced by half. Set aside to cool. Put the lychees in a blender or food processor and work to a purée. For a smooth sorbet you will have to press the purée through a sieve. Put the purée in a measuring jug and add enough of the syrup to make 450 ml/3/4 pint (2 cups). Stir in 3 or 4 teaspoons rose water and 2 or 3 drops cochineal – be careful, the sorbet must be the palest pink. Pour the purée into a rigid container, cover and put in the freezer. After about 2 hours, when the mixture is beginning to freeze, remove the container from the freezer. Using a hand-held electric beater, whisk 2 large egg whites until stiff, then whisk them into the lychee purée. Return the mixture to the freezer. Beat again after 1 1/2 to 2 hours, then freeze for at least 4 hours before serving. Serve with fresh seeded lychees, if available.

C · O · U · N · T · D · O · W · N

The day before:
Put the lamb cubes in a bowl and mix in the marinade. Cover with cling film (plastic wrap) and store in the refrigerator.

On the day:
Cook the prawn curry; do not garnish. Cool, cover and refrigerate. Prepare the spiced spinach, cool, cover and refrigerate. Prepare the tomatoes with ginger, and green beans with coconut, cool, cover and refrigerate.

To serve at 8 pm:
5.30: Take the marinated lamb out of the refrigerator and allow to come to room temperature.
6.30: Cut the green pepper into squares, quarter the onions and separate the layers. Thread the meat, pepper and onions on to eight skewers.
7.00: Heat the barbecue, if using.
7.30: Preheat the grill (broiler) to very hot, if using. Grill or barbecue the kebabs.
7.40: Reheat the curry, spinach, tomato and green bean dishes.
8.00: Garnish the kebabs and curry. Serve.

F · R · E · E · Z · E · R · N · O · T · E · S

Cook the Spiced Spinach, cool quickly, then spoon into a rigid container. Cover, seal and freeze for up to 6 months. To serve, reheat gently from frozen.

⠿M·E·N·U⠿

· 12 ·

Make-ahead Meal for 4

Lamb Korma
Spinach with Yellow Mung Beans
Pilau Rice
Semolina Halwa

Most Indian meals end simply with fresh fruit. Mangoes are a great favourite, or try papaya, water melon or guavas. Sweets are mainly reserved for special occasions. Indian sweets and sweetmeats are usually very sweet and often based on condensed milk, which can be kept for long periods without refrigeration. The halwa in this menu is a delightful sweetmeat made from semolina and coconut and flavoured with cardamom.

Spice Wise

The poppy seeds in the korma recipe are the cream coloured seeds (*khus-khus*) of the Asian poppy, not the blue-grey seeds of the European variety. They are used whole in a number of vegetable dishes, and crushed or ground in kormas and other curried dishes. Asafetida (*hing*) is a large pungent plant, a member of the parsley family, which is native to Afghanistan, northern India and the Middle East. The spice is prepared from the sap and is indeed evil-smelling. Asafetida is available in lump and powdered form only from Asian grocers. It is used in minute quantities and is supposed to enhance the flavour of other spices. It is usually added first to very hot oil and sautéed for a second before the other spices and ingredients are added. Buy the powdered form only and keep it in an airtight container.

Cumin seeds resemble caraway seeds, but the flavour is not quite as palatable. Available ground or whole, they keep better in the latter form.

Lamb Korma

Metric/Imperial	American
150 ml/¼ pint natural yogurt	²/₃ cup unflavored yogurt
1 tablespoon creamed coconut	1 tablespoon creamed coconut
3 cloves garlic, peeled and crushed	3 cloves garlic, peeled and crushed
1 × 2.5 cm/1 inch piece fresh root ginger, peeled and grated	1 × 1 inch piece fresh gingerroot, peeled and grated
1 tablespoon poppy seeds, crushed	1 tablespoon poppy seeds, crushed
2 tablespoons coriander seeds, crushed	2 tablespoons coriander seeds, crushed
1 × 2.5 cm/1 inch piece cinnamon stick, crushed	1 × 1 inch piece cinnamon stick, crushed
6 cloves, crushed	6 cloves, crushed
125 g/4 oz ghee (page 8) or butter	½ cup ghee (page 8) or butter
5 onions, thinly sliced	5 onions, thinly sliced
750 g/1½ lb lean lamb, trimmed and cut into 2.5 cm/1 inch cubes	1½ lb lean lamb, trimmed and cut into 1 inch cubes
1 green chilli, seeded and finely sliced	1 green chili, seeded and finely sliced
juice of ½ lemon	juice of ½ lemon
fresh coriander leaves or parsley, to garnish	fresh coriander leaves or parsley, to garnish

1. Put the yogurt in a small bowl and whisk with a fork until smooth.

2. Put the creamed coconut, garlic, ginger, poppy seeds, coriander seeds, cinnamon and cloves in a blender or food processor and work to a paste.

3. Melt the ghee or butter in a large, heavy-based saucepan and stir-fry the onions until crisp and brown. Remove the onions and purée in a blender or food processor or pass through a fine food mill.

4. Add the spice mixture to the same saucepan and cook gently for 5 minutes. Add the cubed meat, puréed onions and yogurt. Bring to the boil, cover and simmer over a low heat for 45 minutes until the meat is tender and the sauce is brown.

5. Add the finely sliced chilli and lemon juice, stir well and simmer for another 5 minutes.

6. Transfer to a warm serving dish and serve garnished with fresh coriander or parsley. ·5·

Spinach with Yellow Mung Beans

Metric/Imperial	American
75 g/3 oz plain or chick pea flour (besan)	¾ cup all-purpose or chick pea flour (besan)
½ teaspoon ground turmeric	½ teaspoon ground turmeric
1.25 litres/2¼ pints water	5½ cups water
250 ml/8 fl oz natural yogurt	1 cup unflavored yogurt
2 tablespoons yellow mung beans	2 tablespoons yellow mung beans
750 g/1½ lb fresh spinach, washed, shaken dry and roughly chopped	1½ lb fresh spinach, washed, shaken dry and roughly chopped
2½ teaspoons salt	2½ teaspoons salt
2 tablespoons lemon juice	2 tablespoons lemon juice
½ teaspoon cayenne	½ teaspoon cayenne
freshly ground black pepper	freshly ground black pepper
2 tablespoons oil	2 tablespoons oil
½ teaspoon asafetida powder	½ teaspoon asafetida powder
1 teaspoon cumin seeds	1 teaspoon cumin seeds
2 dried red chillis, seeded and crushed	2 dried red chilis, seeded and crushed

1. Sift the flour and turmeric into a bowl. Gradually stir in 4 tablespoons of the water to give a smooth paste.

2. In another bowl, whisk the yogurt until smooth, then gradually stir in the remaining water.

3. Beat the flour mixture together with the yogurt mixture. Pour into a 4½ litre/7½ pint saucepan and bring to the boil over gentle heat. Add the mung beans, spinach, salt, lemon juice and cayenne. Bring back to the boil, reduce the heat and simmer very gently for 1½ hours, stirring every 10 minutes. If the mixture gets too thick, thin with a little hot water to the consistency of pea soup.

4. Taste and adjust the seasoning, then cover and keep warm.

5. Heat the oil in a small frying pan (skillet). Add the asafetida, then 2 seconds later the cumin, then 2 seconds later the chillis. As soon as the chillis darken, stir, wait for a second and stir once again. Pour the sizzling hot spices over the mixture in the saucepan. Cover the pan and leave until the sizzling stops. Serve at once. ·7·

Lamb korma; Sour-sweet chick peas (page 11); Spinach with yellow mung beans

Pilau Rice

Metric/Imperial	American
75 g/3 oz ghee (page 8) or butter	6 tablespoons ghee (page 8) or butter
1 small onion, chopped	1 small onion, chopped
350 g/12 oz basmati or long-grain rice	2 cups basmati or long-grain rice
1 teaspoon salt	1 teaspoon salt
450 ml/¾ pint water	2 cups water

1. Wash the rice and soak in cold water for 30 minutes, then drain thoroughly.

2. Heat the ghee or butter in a large saucepan and sauté the onion until golden brown. Add the rice and salt, and sauté for 30 seconds to 1 minute.

3. Add the water, cover and bring to the boil. Lower the heat and gently stir the rice a few times. Cover and cook over a very gentle heat for 10 to 15 minutes until the water is fully absorbed and the rice is

cooked. Do not stir during the cooking. If the rice is not cooked by the time the water is fully absorbed, add 1 tablespoon warm water and continue cooking until the rice is tender.

Semolina Halwa

Metric/Imperial	American
250 g/8 oz semolina	1 1/3 cups semolina flour
4 tablespoons desiccated coconut	4 tablespoons shredded coconut
500 g/1 lb sugar	2 cups sugar
1 tablespoon poppy seeds	1 tablespoon poppy seeds
6 cardamoms, shelled and seeds reserved	6 cardamoms, shelled and seeds reserved
600 ml/1 pint water	2 1/2 cups water
125 g/4 oz ghee (page 8) or butter, melted	1/2 cup ghee (page 8) or butter, melted

1. Put the semolina in a heavy saucepan with the coconut, sugar, poppy and cardamom seeds. Mix well, then stir in the water.

2. Bring to the boil, stirring, then lower the heat and simmer for at least 1 hour, stirring frequently, until every ingredient is soft. Add the ghee or butter gradually and mix well.

3. Transfer the mixture to a shallow tray and spread evenly; cool. Cut into triangle or diamond shapes. Store the Semolina Halwa in an airtight container in a cool place.

Optional Extra:
For a refreshing end to this spicy meal make a tropical fruit salad using fresh dates, mangoes, lychees, paw-paws, kiwi and sharon fruit, or any other exotic fruit you like. Decorate with toasted almonds and slices of fresh coconut (you can get these frozen from South-East Asian shops).

C · O · U · N · T · D · O · W · N

The day before:
Cook the lamb korma, but do not add the last 3 ingredients. Cool, cover and refrigerate. Make the spinach dish, but do not add the last 4 ingredients. Cool, cover and refrigerate. Make the chick peas, but do not add the fresh chillis and ginger. Cool, cover and store in the refrigerator. Make the halwa and keep in an airtight container in a cool place.

On the day:
Make the pilau rice. When cooked, turn into an ovenproof serving dish. Cover tightly with foil and a lid.

To serve at 8 pm:
6.00: Take the lamb and vegetable dishes out of the refrigerator. Set aside and leave to come to room temperature.
7.10: Preheat the oven to 180°C/350°F, Gas Mark 4.
About 7.20: Gently reheat the lamb and vegetable dishes on top of the cooker. Add the chilli and lemon juice to the korma.
7.30: Reheat the pilau in the oven.
7.40: Sauté the asafetida, cumin seeds and chillis and pour into the spinach. Add the chillis and ginger to the chick peas. Arrange the halwa on a serving dish.
8.00: Garnish the dishes and take the savoury ones to the table.

F · R · E · E · Z · E · R · N · O · T · E · S

Make the Lamb Korma, without the chilli, lemon juice and garnish. Cool quickly, remove any fat from the top, and spoon into a rigid container. Cover, seal and freeze for up to 2 months. To serve, thaw at room temperature, then heat gently. Add the chilli and lemon juice, and garnish. Make the spinach without the final sautéed spices. Cool quickly and turn into a rigid container. Cover, seal and freeze for up to 3 months. To serve, thaw at room temperature, then heat gently. Add the sautéed asafetida, cumin seeds and chillis. Make the chick peas, without the chilli and ginger. Cool quickly and turn into a rigid container. Cover, seal and freeze for up to 3 months. To serve, thaw at room temperature, then heat gently. Add the chilli and ginger.

⁙M⧫E⧫N⧫U⁙

· 13 ·

Easy Entertaining for 4

Curried Steak
or
Meatball Curry
Aubergines and Tomatoes
Cabbage with Green Peppers
Apple Chutney

Choice of Main Dish

Choosing an Indian menu when entertaining will always give that exotic touch to the occasion. There is a choice of main dishes in this menu. The curried steak is unusual in Indian cooking because the meat is expensive rump, or other frying steak, instead of the usual stewing variety. As a result the curry is quickly made yet still delicious. If you do not want to put too much of a strain on the budget, select the meatball curry (*kofta*), less expensive, but just as tasty. Both recipes require a wok or deep frying pan (skillet).

The accompanying vegetable dishes contrast in colour, texture and taste, providing a perfect balance with either meat curry. Serve with plain boiled rice (page 36) or *chapatis* (page 62).

Indian Chutneys

The other accompaniment to this menu is apple chutney. Chutneys play an important part in an Indian meal. Some are hot, others are mild. There are two main types: uncooked, which need to be consumed within a few days, and cooked, which keep well in sealed jars. There are no strict rules regarding which type of chutney to serve with a specific food – just please yourself.

Curried Steak

Metric/Imperial	American
1½ teaspoons ground coriander	1½ teaspoons ground coriander
1 teaspoon ground turmeric	1 teaspoon ground turmeric
1 teaspoon ground cumin	1 teaspoon ground cumin
1½ teaspoons salt	1½ teaspoons salt
1 teaspoon freshly ground black pepper	1 teaspoon freshly ground black pepper
1 tablespoon milk	1 tablespoon milk
50 g/2 oz ghee (page 8) or 2 tablespoons oil	¼ cup ghee (page 8) or 2 tablespoons oil
1 small onion, sliced	1 small onion, sliced
1 clove garlic, peeled and sliced	1 clove garlic, peeled and sliced
500 g/1 lb good quality steak, cut into 2.5 cm/ 1 inch cubes	1 lb good quality steak, cut into 1 inch cubes
120 ml/4 fl oz water	½ cup water
chopped mint, to garnish	chopped mint, to garnish

1. Mix the coriander, turmeric, cumin, salt and pepper to a paste with the milk. Heat the ghee or oil in a wok or deep frying pan (skillet) and sauté the onion and garlic until soft. Stir in the paste and cook for a further 1 minute. Push to one side of the saucepan.
2. Add the steak and stir-fry until browned on all sides. Stir in the water and bring to the boil. Simmer for 3 minutes. Sprinkle the Curried Steak with mint; serve hot. ·8·

Optional Extra

Serve a raita, including a fresh mango or pineapple. Peel and cube a fresh mango or small pineapple. Stir it into 500 ml/1 pint (2½ cups) natural (unflavored) yogurt. Add a little salt and a finely chopped, seeded green chilli. Heat 1 tablespoon oil in a small frying pan (skillet) and sauté 1 teaspoon mustard seeds for a few seconds. When the seeds begin to change colour and splutter, pour them and the oil into the raita.

Meatball Curry

Metric/Imperial	American
500 g/1 lb minced beef	1 lb ground beef
2 large onions, finely chopped	2 large onions, finely chopped
4 cloves garlic, peeled and finely chopped	4 cloves garlic, peeled and finely chopped
2 teaspoons ground turmeric	2 teaspoons ground turmeric
2 teaspoons chilli powder	2 teaspoons chili powder
2 teaspoons ground coriander	2 teaspoons ground coriander
1½ teaspoons ground cumin	1½ teaspoons ground cumin
1 teaspoon ground ginger	1 teaspoon ground ginger
freshly ground black pepper	freshly ground black pepper
2 teaspoons salt	2 teaspoons salt
1 egg, beaten	1 egg, beaten
oil, for deep-frying	oil, for deep-frying
125 g/4 oz ghee (page 8) or 4 tablespoons oil	½ cup ghee (page 8) or ¼ cup oil
200 ml/⅓ pint water	1 cup water
mint leaves, to garnish	mint leaves, to garnish

1. Put the beef in a bowl and add half the onions, garlic, spices and salt. Stir well, then bind the mixture together with the beaten egg.
2. Form the mixture into small balls. Heat the oil in a wok or deep-fryer and fry the meatballs, a few at a time, for 5 minutes. Remove from the pan with a slotted spoon, drain on absorbent kitchen paper and set aside. Pour the oil from the wok and wipe it out.
3. Heat the ghee or oil in the wok, or a deep frying pan or saucepan, and sauté the remaining onions and garlic until soft. Add the remaining spices and salt and stir-fry for a further 3 minutes. Add the meatballs and gently coat with the spices. Pour in the water and bring to the boil. Lower the heat and simmer gently for 30 minutes. Serve hot, garnished with mint leaves. ·3·

Aubergines and tomatoes

Aubergines and Tomatoes

Metric/Imperial

175 g/6 oz ghee (page 8) or
    4 tablespoons oil
1 large onion, sliced
2 cloves garlic, peeled and
    sliced
1 teaspoon ground coriander
1 × 2.5 cm/1 inch
    cinnamon stick
1 teaspoon chilli powder
1 teaspoon salt
1 teaspoon freshly ground
    black pepper
500 g/1 lb aubergines, cut
    into 2.5 cm/1 inch pieces
500 g/1 lb tomatoes, cut
    into 2.5 cm/1 inch pieces
3 tablespoons tomato purée
200 ml/⅓ pint water

American

¾ cup ghee (page 8) or
    ¼ cup oil
1 large onion, sliced
2 cloves garlic, peeled and
    sliced
1 teaspoon ground coriander
1 × 1 inch cinnamon stick
1 teaspoon chili powder
1 teaspoon salt
1 teaspoon freshly ground
    black pepper
1 lb eggplant, cut into
    1 inch pieces
1 lb tomatoes, cut into
    1 inch pieces
3 tablespoons tomato paste
1 cup water

1. Heat the ghee or oil in a wok or deep frying pan and sauté the onion and garlic until soft. Add the spices and seasonings and stir-fry for 3 minutes.
2. Add the aubergines (eggplant), tomatoes and tomato purée (paste) and toss gently to coat with the spice mixture.
3. Stir in the water and bring to the boil. Lower the heat and simmer for 25 to 30 minutes or until the aubergines are tender and the sauce is quite thick. Increase the heat to boil off any excess liquid, if necessary. Serve hot.

Cabbage with Green Peppers

Metric/Imperial

3 tablespoons oil
1 large onion, thinly sliced
1 × 2.5 cm/1 inch piece
    fresh root ginger, peeled
    and cut into fine
    matchsticks
2 cloves garlic, peeled and
    cut into fine matchsticks
2 green chillis, seeded and
    chopped
1 teaspoon fennel seeds
2 large green peppers, seeded
    and sliced
1 green cabbage, shredded
salt
freshly ground black pepper

American

3 tablespoons oil
1 large onion, thinly sliced
1 × 1 inch piece fresh
    gingerroot, peeled and
    cut into fine matchsticks
2 cloves garlic, peeled and
    cut into fine matchsticks
2 green chilis, seeded and
    chopped
1 teaspoon fennel seeds
2 large green peppers, seeded
    and sliced
1 green cabbage, shredded
salt
freshly ground black pepper

1. Heat the oil in a large saucepan and sauté the onion until golden. Add the ginger, garlic, chillis and fennel seeds and stir-fry for 1 minute.
2. Add the green pepper and stir-fry for 2 minutes. Put in the cabbage and salt and pepper to taste. Stir well and cook until the cabbage softens slightly. Continue cooking, uncovered, for 10 minutes. ·10·

Apple Chutney

Metric/Imperial	American
1.25 kg/2½ lb cooking apples, peeled and cored	*2½ lb tart apples, peeled and cored*
1 tablespoon salt	*1 tablespoon salt*
500 ml/18 fl oz vinegar	*2 cups vinegar*
300 g/10 oz soft brown sugar	*1⅔ cups firmly packed brown sugar*
125 g/4 oz raisins	*⅔ cup raisins*
125 g/4 oz sultanas	*⅔ cup golden raisins*
½ teaspoon mustard seeds	*½ teaspoon mustard seeds*
25 g/1 oz fresh root ginger, peeled and sliced	*1 oz fresh gingerroot, peeled and sliced*
1-2 cloves garlic, peeled and chopped	*1-2 cloves garlic, peeled and chopped*
1 teaspoon chilli powder	*1 teaspoon chili powder*

1. Slice the apples and lay them on a dish. Sprinkle with half the salt, cover and set aside.
2. Place half the vinegar in a saucepan, add the sugar and stir over a low heat until the sugar has dissolved. Bring to the boil and boil for 5 minutes or until the syrup is thick. Allow to cool.
3. Place the remaining vinegar in a pan, add the apples and simmer for 3 to 4 minutes until tender. Allow to cool.
4. Stir the vinegar syrup, raisins, sultanas (golden raisins), mustard seeds, remaining salt, ginger, garlic and chilli powder into the apples.
5. Bottle the chutney in airtight jars with vinegar-proof tops. Leave to mature for 4 to 5 weeks before eating. ·7·

Optional Extra

Try a green bean pickle that goes equally well with Indian or western food – leave out the chillis if you like and serve with roast meat or chicken. Put 500 g/1 lb topped and tailed (trimmed) green beans in a saucepan of boiling salted water. Cook for 3 minutes, then drain and refresh under cold running water. Leave to drain in the colander. Meanwhile put 600 ml/1 pint (2½ cups) white wine vinegar in a saucepan with 1 thinly sliced onion, 3 halved cloves garlic, 75 g/3 oz (⅓ cup) sugar, 1 teaspoon salt, 2 or 3 crumbled dried red chillis, 2 bay leaves and 1 teaspoon fennel seeds. Bring to the boil, cover the pan and simmer very gently for 30 minutes. Stand the beans upright in two 500 g/1 lb jam jars. Strain the vinegar and pour into the jars. The vinegar should cover the beans; if there is not enough, top up with some plain vinegar. Cover the jars tightly and leave to cool. This pickle is also good made with long green chillis – but only for those with hardened palates.

C · O · U · N · T · D · O · W · N

About 4 weeks before:
Make the Apple Chutney, bottle and store in a cool place.

The day before:
If making the meatball curry, cook, cool, cover and refrigerate. Prepare the aubergines and tomatoes. Cool, cover and refrigerate.

On the day:
Prepare the curried steak if making. Prepare the vegetables for the cabbage with green peppers, cover and refrigerate.

To serve at 8 pm:
7.30: Gently reheat the meatball curry or curried steak and the aubergines and tomatoes.
7.40: Cook the cabbage with green peppers. Spoon the chutney into a small dish.
8.00: Garnish the curry. Take the dishes to the table.

F · R · E · E · Z · E · R · N · O · T · E · S

Make the curried steak or meatball curry. Cool quickly and skim off any fat from the top. Spoon the curry into a rigid container. Cover, seal and freeze for up to 2 months. To serve, thaw at room temperature and heat gently until very hot. Make the aubergines and tomatoes. Cool quickly and spoon into a rigid container. Cover, seal and freeze for up to 3 months.

⸚M·E·N·U⸚

· 14 ·

Summer Evening Meal for 4

Fish in Coconut Milk
Lamb Curry
Sour Aubergines
Spinach and Potato
Kulfi

When serving spicy Indian food on a warm summer evening, make sure you have plenty of chilled soft drinks and beer, or make a fruit punch.

Serving Rice with a Difference

A traditional and attractive way to serve plain boiled rice is to press it into small individual bowls (*katori*), then tap them out on to the dinner plate in small mounds. The lamb curry and the vegetable dishes can be served with *chapatis* or *naans* (pages 62 or 63).

Traditional Kulfi

A refreshing finale to an Indian meal, particularly in the summer, is *kulfi* – ice cream made with milk that has been reduced by between one-third and one-half by simmering – to which is added a kind of condensed milk called *khoia* (made by simmering milk until it is reduced to thick sludge). However, in this recipe the *khoia* is replaced by cream – *khoia* is tedious to make and usually left to the professionals. Nuts and sugar, and sometimes essences, are added for flavouring. Traditionally *kulfi* is set in small cone-shaped metal moulds (molds). The filled moulds are put into earthenware pots or buckets filled with ice chips, salt and saltpetre. The pot or bucket is then rotated by hand until the ice cream sets. Another tedious process, not to be attempted by the amateur.

Fish in Coconut Milk

Metric/Imperial

4 cod cutlets or steaks, 3
cm/1¼ inches thick
3 tablespoons oil
1 teaspoon mustard seeds
2 onions, finely sliced
2 cloves garlic, peeled and
crushed
2 green chillis, seeded and
finely chopped
1 × 1 cm/½ inch piece
fresh root ginger, peeled
and finely grated
1 green pepper, seeded and
thinly sliced
1 tablespoon cornflour

American

4 cod cutlets or steaks, 1¼
inches thick
3 tablespoons oil
1 teaspoon mustard seeds
2 onions, finely sliced
2 cloves garlic, peeled and
crushed
2 green chilis, seeded and
finely chopped
1 × ½ inch piece fresh
gingerroot, peeled and
finely grated
1 green pepper, seeded and
thinly sliced
1 tablespoon cornstarch

300 ml/½ pint coconut
milk (page 42)
½ teaspoon salt
1 tablespoon desiccated
coconut, lightly toasted
2 tablespoons lemon juice
fresh coriander, to garnish

1¼ cups coconut milk
(page 42)
½ teaspoon salt
1 tablespoon shredded
coconut, lightly toasted
2 tablespoons lemon juice
fresh coriander, to garnish

1. Pat the cod steaks dry with absorbent kitchen paper. Heat the oil in a large frying pan (skillet) and sauté the mustard seeds. As soon as they jump, add the onions, garlic, chillis and ginger, and sauté over gentle heat for 3 to 4 minutes until beginning to soften. Add the green pepper and cook for 2 to 3 minutes. Add the cornflour (cornstarch) and stir.

Lamb curry; Kashmiri pilau (page 35); Fish in coconut milk; Sour aubergines

2. Stir in the coconut milk and salt. Stir and bring slowly to the boil over a low heat.

3. Add the cod to the pan. Spoon over the sauce, cover and simmer very gently for 15 to 20 minutes or until the fish is cooked and flakes easily.

4. Sprinkle the toasted coconut and lemon juice over the fish. Garnish with the coriander leaves. ·10·

Lamb Curry

Metric/Imperial	American
1 tablespoon oil or butter	1 tablespoon oil or butter
1 onion, finely chopped	1 onion, finely chopped
2 cloves garlic, peeled and crushed	2 cloves garlic, peeled and crushed
2 fresh green chillis, seeded and sliced	2 fresh green chilis, seeded and sliced
2 teaspoons chilli powder	2 teaspoons chili powder
500 g/1 lb boned leg of lamb, cut into 4 cm/1½ inch cubes	1 lb boned leg of lamb, cut into 1½ inch cubes
1 tablespoon vinegar	1 tablespoon vinegar
salt	salt
2 tomatoes, peeled, seeded and chopped	2 tomatoes, peeled, seeded and chopped
2 teaspoons garam masala (page 37)	2 teaspoons garam masala (page 37)
1 tablespoon desiccated coconut	1 tablespoon shredded coconut

1. Heat the oil or butter in a heavy-based frying pan (skillet) and sauté the onion, garlic, fresh chillis and chilli powder for 2 minutes. Add the lamb, vinegar, salt to taste and tomatoes. Stir thoroughly.

2. Cover the pan and cook over moderate heat for 30 to 45 minutes or until the lamb is tender. Add a little water or lemon juice if the curry looks too dry or is sticking. Add the garam masala and cook for a further 5 minutes.

3. Transfer to a warm serving dish, scatter with coconut and serve with Kashmiri Pilau (page 35). ·11·

Sour Aubergines

Metric/Imperial	American
500 g/1 lb aubergines, halved lengthways and cut into thin slices	1 lb eggplant, halved lengthwise and cut into thin slices
salt	salt
4 tablespoons oil	4 tablespoons oil
2 teaspoons ground fennel seeds	2 teaspoons ground fennel seeds
½ teaspoon ground ginger	½ teaspoon ground ginger
1 teaspoon ground cumin	1 teaspoon ground cumin
½ teaspoon ground turmeric	½ teaspoon ground turmeric
½ teaspoon cayenne	½ teaspoon cayenne
½ teaspoon asafetida powder (page 49) (optional)	½ teaspoon asafetida powder (page 49) (optional)
350 ml/12 fl oz water	1½ cups water
1 tablespoon tamarind paste (page 9)	1 tablespoon tamarind paste (page 9)

1. Sprinkle the aubergines (eggplant) with 2 tablespoons salt and leave to drain in a colander for 30 minutes. Rinse the aubergine slices and pat dry with absorbent kitchen paper.

2. Heat the oil in a large frying pan (skillet) and sauté half the aubergine slices in a single layer until reddish brown. Turn and cook on the other side. Remove the aubergine slices with a slotted spoon and drain. Sauté the remaining aubergine slices in the same way.

3. Combine the fennel seeds with the ginger, cumin, turmeric and cayenne. Add the asafetida to the pan, if using, then the spice mixture and 2 tablespoons of the water. Stir for 30 seconds over gentle heat, then add a further 2 tablespoons water and stir for a further 10 seconds. Add the tamarind, salt to taste and the remaining water.

4. Return the aubergines to the pan and bring to the boil. Turn the aubergines in the sauce, cover the pan, lower the heat and cook gently for 5 minutes. ·2·

Spinach and Potato

Metric/Imperial	American
40 g/1½ oz ghee (page 8) or butter	3 tablespoons ghee (page 8) or butter
250 g/8 oz potatoes, peeled and cut into chunks	½ lb potatoes, peeled and cut into chunks
2 cloves garlic, peeled and crushed	2 cloves garlic, peeled and crushed
2 teaspoons grated fresh root ginger	2 teaspoons grated fresh gingerroot
1 green chilli, halved and seeded	1 green chili, halved and seeded
500 g/1 lb fresh spinach, roughly chopped, or 250 g/8 oz frozen chopped spinach	1 lb fresh spinach, roughly chopped, or ½ lb frozen chopped spinach
2-3 sprigs coriander leaves, chopped	2-3 sprigs coriander leaves, chopped

1. Heat the ghee or butter in a saucepan and sauté the potatoes for 4 to 5 minutes. Add the garlic, ginger and chilli, and sauté for 1 to 2 minutes.
2. Stir in the spinach and coriander leaves. Continue to sauté for 10 to 15 minutes until the potatoes are tender and the spinach is dry. Add a little water if the mixture becomes too dry during cooking. ·2·

Kulfi

Metric/Imperial	American
900 ml/1½ pints milk	3¾ cups milk
50 g/2 oz rice flour	½ cup rice flour
300 ml/½ pint double cream	1¼ cups heavy cream
125 g/4 oz sugar	½ cup sugar
1 tablespoon chopped pistachio nuts	1 tablespoon chopped pistachio nuts
1 tablespoon chopped blanched almonds	1 tablespoon chopped blanched almonds
pistachio nuts, to decorate	pistachio nuts, to decorate

1. Bring the milk to the boil in a heavy-based saucepan. Lower the heat and simmer, uncovered, until the milk is reduced to two-thirds.
2. Gradually stir in the rice flour, then the cream. Bring to the boil again, then lower the heat and simmer for a further 15 minutes. Add the sugar, stirring well to dissolve.
3. Leave to cool, then stir in the nuts. Transfer the mixture to freezing containers and freeze until partially frozen.
4. Remove from the freezer and beat the mixture vigorously to break down the ice crystals. Freeze again until firm. Decorate with pistachio nuts. ·12·

C · O · U · N · T · D · O · W · N

The day before:
Make the *kulfi* and freeze.
On the day:
Prepare the lamb curry, without the garam masala and coconut, the sour aubergines and the spinach and potato. Cool the dishes, cover and refrigerate.
To serve at 8 pm:
7.00: Make the coconut milk sauce for the fish.
7.30: Cook the fish.
7.40: Reheat the lamb curry, adding the garam masala and coconut. Reheat the sour aubergines and the spinach and potatoes.
7.45: Take the *kulfi* out of the freezer, decorate and place in the refrigerator.
8.00: Garnish the dishes and serve.

F · R · E · E · Z · E · R · N · O · T · E · S

Cook the lamb curry. Cool quickly and skim off any fat from the top. Turn into a rigid container, cover, seal and freeze for up to 2 months. To serve, thaw at room temperature for 3 to 4 hours. Heat gently, adding a little water if the mixture is too dry. Cook the sour aubergines. Cool quickly and skim off any fat from the top. Spoon into a rigid container, cover, seal and freeze for up to 3 months. To serve, thaw at room temperature for 4 hours, then heat gently.

Traditional Indian Breads

Chapati
Puri
Paratha
Naan

There are several types of Indian bread. Most are flat, usually unleavened and mainly used in India to pick up food. A small piece is torn off, wrapped around some food and neatly popped into the mouth. Elegant Indian eaters will hardly soil their fingers in the process. The most commonly used flour is a finely ground wholewheat (*ata*). *Ata* is available from most Indian and Pakistani grocers, but any stoneground wholewheat flour will produce an acceptable result.

Chapatis are the simplest of all breads, needing only flour and water. Puris are made with a similar dough but with a little fat and salt added. A traditional Indian breakfast will often include puris; they are eaten simply with spicy potatoes and plenty of chutney. Paratha is essentially a fried chapati. A good paratha depends on the layering of fat in the dough.

Cooking Methods

Several methods of cooking are used for the variety of breads served with Indian meals. Convex griddles (*tawas*) are used to cook the dry fried doughs such as chapatis and wok-like *karhais* used for bread fried in ghee such as roti. Traditional clay ovens are used to bake the popular leavened naan breads. The act of slapping the rounds of dough on to the searing walls of the oven is an art in itself, as is knowing when to hook them out again! However an acceptable naan can be produced from a very hot conventional oven.

The dough of all the breads must be well-kneaded until soft and pliable. Traditionally, kneading is done with the fists. Most Indian kitchens do not have tables or worktops: all the work is done squatting on the floor and the dough is worked in a metal tray or pan. A small round wooden board and a thin wooden rolling pin, rather like a stick, are used to roll out the bread.

Chapati

Metric/Imperial
250 g/8 oz ata (page 61)
1/2 teaspoon salt
about 200 ml/1/3 pint
    water

American
2 cups ata (page 61)
1/2 teaspoon salt
about 1 cup water

1. Sift the flour and salt into a bowl. Add the water gradually and mix to a firm dough. Turn on to a lightly floured surface and knead well until smooth and elastic.
2. Break the dough into 8 to 10 pieces, then form into balls. Roll out on a lightly floured surface as thinly as possible, the dough must be less than 3 mm/1/8 inch thick.
3. Heat a frying pan (skillet) and when it is very hot turn the heat down. Put a chapati in the pan and cook for 3 to 4 minutes until blisters begin to appear. Turn the chapati over and cook the other side for 3 to 4 minutes. (If liked, remove the chapati from the pan with tongs, then place directly on the heat and cook for a few seconds until black blisters form and the chapati swells up.) Keep the chapatis hot in the oven or under the grill (broiler) while cooking the remainder.
4. Serve hot as soon as possible after cooking. Makes 8 to 10.

Puri

Metric/Imperial
175 g/6 oz ata (page 61)
1/2 teaspoon salt
150 ml/1/4 pint water
50 g/2 oz melted ghee (page
    8) or butter
oil, for deep-frying

American
1 1/2 cups ata (page 61)
1/2 teaspoon salt
2/3 cup water
1/4 cup melted ghee (page
    8) or butter
oil, for deep-frying

1. Sift the flour and salt into a bowl. Add the water gradually to make a firm dough. Add the ghee or butter, kneading it in well, then rest for 20 minutes.

Puris; Chapatis; Parathas

2. Break the dough into 8 to 10 pieces, approximately 2.5 cm/1 inch in diameter, then form each piece into a ball. Roll out on a lightly floured surface into neat rounds, each just less than 3 mm/⅛ inch thick.

3. Heat the oil in a deep-fryer until moderately hot. Deep-fry the puris, one at a time, for about 1½ minutes until they puff up and float to the surface, spooning the oil over them as they fry. Remove from the pan and drain on absorbent kitchen paper. Keep hot while deep-frying the remaining puris.

4. Serve hot. Makes 8 to 10.

Paratha

Metric/Imperial	American
250 g/8 oz ata (page 61)	2 cups ata (page 61)
½ teaspoon salt	½ teaspoon salt
200 ml/⅓ pint water	1 cup water
125 g/4 oz melted ghee (page 8) or butter	½ cup melted ghee (page 8) or butter

1. Sift the flour and salt into a bowl. Add the water gradually and mix to a firm dough. Turn on to a lightly floured surface and knead well until smooth and elastic.

2. Break the dough into 4 to 6 pieces and roll into balls, approximately 7.5 cm/3 inches in diameter. Roll each out on a lightly floured surface to a 3 mm/⅛ inch thickness.

3. Brush with melted ghee or butter, then roll up from one side and re-form into a ball. Repeat this rolling process five times, then roll out to a 5 mm/¼ inch thickness.

4. Warm a lightly greased frying pan (skillet) over high heat, place a paratha in the pan and cook over moderate heat for about 1 to 1½ minutes on each side until lightly browned. Keep hot in the oven or under the grill (broiler) while cooking the remainder.

5. Serve hot, as soon as possible after cooking. Makes 4 to 6.

Naan

Metric/Imperial	American
250 g/8 oz plain flour	2 cups all-purpose flour
½ teaspoon baking powder	½ teaspoon baking powder
1 teaspoon salt	1 teaspoon salt
1 teaspoon sugar	1 teaspoon sugar
1 teaspoon dried yeast	1 teaspoon active dry yeast
150 ml/¼ pint milk	⅔ cup milk
150 ml/¼ pint natural yogurt	⅔ cup unflavored yogurt
1 egg, beaten	1 egg, beaten
2 teaspoons poppy seeds (optional)	2 teaspoons poppy seeds (optional)

1. Sift the flour, baking powder, salt and sugar into a bowl. Mix the yeast to a paste with a little of the milk. Beat the yogurt into the remaining milk and heat until lukewarm. Stir in the yeast paste. Add this mixture gradually to the flour and mix to a dough. Knead well, then add the egg and knead again. Cover the dough with a damp cloth and leave in a warm place for 1½ hours or until doubled in size.

2. Put the baking sheets in a preheated oven (230°C/450°F), Gas Mark 8 while you shape the dough. Break the dough into 6 to 8 pieces, approximately 6 cm/2½ inches in diameter. Roll into balls and flatten with the hand into an oval shape. Press the poppy seeds, if using, into the naan.

3. Place on the baking sheets and bake for 12 minutes or until the naan are puffed and blistered.

4. Serve hot. Makes 6 to 8.

F · R · E · E · Z · E · R · N · O · T · E · S

Cook and cool chapatis, parathas, naans and besani roti. Open freeze, then pack in polythene (plastic) bags. Seal and freeze for up to 2 months. To serve, heat straight from the freezer in a preheated oven (180°C/350°F), Gas Mark 4 until very hot. Alternatively, freeze the bread dough. Thaw at room temperature until soft and pliable.

I · N · D · E · X

A·C·K·N·O·W·L·E·D·G·E·M·E·N·T·S

Bryce Atwell 7, 10, 15, 18, 23, 27, 31, 34, 39; Laurie Evans 51, 58; Robert Golden 42, 46, 55, 62.

Jacket photography: Clive Streeter   Illustration: Catherine Denvir